D1598233

IMAGES OF SANCTITY IN EDDIUS STEPHANUS' *LIFE OF BISHOP WILFRID*, AN EARLY ENGLISH SAINT'S LIFE

William Trent Foley

The Edwin Mellen Press
Lewiston/Queenston/Lampeter

Library of Congress Cataloging-in-Publication Data

Foley, William Trent, 1954-
    Images of sanctity in Eddius Stephanus' "Life of Bishop Wilfrid," an
early English saint's life / William Trent Foley.
      p.   cm.
    Includes bibliographical references and index.
    ISBN 0-7734-9513-4
    1. Eddius Stephanus. Vita Wilfridi. 2. Wilfrid, Saint,
Archbishop of York, 634-709--Legends--History and criticism.
I. Title.
BX4700.W5E434   1992
270.2' 092--dc20   92-11976
                                                                   CIP

A CIP catalog record for this book is available
from The British Library.

The Edwin Mellen Press   The Edwin Mellen Press
P.O. Box 450   Box 67
Lewiston, NY 14092   Queenston, Ontario
USA   CANADA L0S 1L0

The Edwin Mellen Press, Ltd.
Lampeter, Dyfed, Wales
UNITED KINGDOM SA48 7DY

Printed in the United States of America

TO THE MEMORY OF
JOHN BUNYAN SPENCER

TABLE OF CONTENTS

The Nature of Religious Convictions and Their Expression
       in Hagiographical Narrative
Internal vs. External History
Hagiography's Theological Dimensions
Saints as Signs
The Nature and Function of Stephen's *Life of Wilfrid*

The Typological Imagination in Paul and in Early Christianity
Stephen's Depiction of Wilfrid as a Type of Christ
The Literary Structure of Stephen's *Life of Wilfrid*
       Predestined (Chapter 1)
       Called (Chapters 2-23)
       Justified (Chapters 24-55)
       Glorified (Chapters 56-68)
A Theology of Persecution and Glorification
Clinging to the Promise: The Apostolic Teaching of the Roman See
Obedient Son and Commanding Father

The Father-Son Dialectic in Stephen's *Life*
The Theological Significance of Wilfrid's Fatherly Role
The Spiritual Father as Teacher
The Spiritual Father as Provider and Protector
The Spiritual Father as a Man of Power

Explanatory Note

Throughout this book, the author of the *Life of Bishop Wilfrid* is designated by Stephen [= Lat. *Stephanus*], the name that the *Life* itself provides, and *not* by Eddius Stephanus, the name that tradition has given to the author, perhaps erroneously.

References to chapter numbers in Stephen's *Life of Wilfrid* follow the numbering scheme in Levison's MGH edition of the *Life*. That numbering scheme is identical to that in Colgrave's Cambridge Press edition, except for chapters 60 and following. Since Colgrave splits what Levison identifies as chapter 60 into two chapters, namely chapters 60 and 61, all subsequent chapter numbers in Colgrave are one higher than in Levison. For example, chapter 63 in the Levison edition is 64 in the Colgrave edition. For the reader's convenience, references to these chapters in the textnotes and footnotes will give both chapter numbers, with the chapter number in the Colgrave edition appearing in parentheses [e.g., LW ch. 63(64)].

Unless otherwise indicated, the passages cited in English from the *Life of Wilfrid* are taken from Colgrave's translation.

In general, ancient and medieval works are designated by their English titles unless there is no published English translation of them, in which case they are designated by their Latin titles.

To avoid ambiguity, the word "Gospel" is capitalized whenever it refers to one of the four canonical Gospels. The words "Life" and "Lives" are likewise capitalized whenever they designate the narrative genre of hagiography. This convention leaves no doubt about the meaning of sentences such as, "Hagiographers narrate the events of saints' lives in saints' Lives."

Unless otherwise noted, all English citations from Scripture are taken from the Revised Standard Version. Chapter and verse citations from the Psalms are numbered according to the Vulgate. To find the corresponding Psalm in the RSV, NEB or other English versions of Scripture, simply augment the number of the Vulgate Psalm by one for all Psalms after Psalm 9.

Abbreviations

AsA	*Acta sancti Annemundi auctore anonymo*
EH	Bede, *The Ecclesiastical History of the English People*
H-S	Edgar Hennecke, Wilhelm Schneemelcher, and R. McL. Wilson, eds., *New Testament Apocrypha*
LA	Bede, *Lives of the Abbots*
LCA	*Anonymous Life of St. Cuthbert*
LCP	Bede, *Prose Life of St. Cuthbert*
LP	*Liber Pontificalis*
LW	Eddius Stephanus, *The Life of Bishop Wilfrid*
LW$_1$	Wilhelm Levison, ed., *Vita Wilfridi I. episcopi Eboracensis auctore Stephano*
LW$_2$	Bertram Colgrave, ed. and trans., *The Life of Bishop Wilfrid*
MGH AA	Monumenta Germaniae Historica--Auctores Antiquissimi
MGH SRM	Monumenta Germaniae Historica--Scriptores Rerum Merovingicarum
OCD	Augustine, *On Christian Doctrine*
OLD	*Oxford Latin Dictionary*, 1982 ed.
PG	J. P. Migne, ed., *Patrologiae Cursus Completus. Series Graeca*
PL	J. P. Migne, ed., *Patrologiae Cursus Completus. Series Latina*
RB	*The Rule of St. Benedict*
RB/1980	Timothy Fry, O.S.B., ed., *RB 1980: The Rule of St. Benedict in Latin and English with Notes*
RM	*The Rule of the Master*
Vg	Latin Vulgate Bible

PREFACE

This study of Stephen's *Life of Bishop Wilfrid* was inspired by recent literary critical trends in biblical research. I have thought for some time that medieval saints' Lives and the New Testament Gospels are genres that, though not identical, resemble each other closely enough to justify using research on one genre to shed light on the other. Whatever else this book might do, I hope at least that it might encourage more discussion between students of hagiography and biblical scholars.

While many New Testament scholars of this century have presupposed that the Gospels were to be used as a means to the larger end of uncovering the Jesus of history, a new generation of scholars has focused upon the Gospels and the evangelists' writing of them as important ends in themselves. By distinguishing between the Jesus of history and the Christ of faith, Rudolf Bultmann and his disciples drew increasing attention to the evangelists' understanding of Jesus as the Christ of God, worthy of one's deepest faith and devotion, and not merely as a prophet or teacher of note, worthy of the historian's remembrance. Convinced that the Gospels offered their readers, above all, the Christ of faith, New Testament scholars soon began to examine the evangelists' separate portrayals of Jesus as the Christ. Inevitably, they came to notice that these portrayals differed from each other not only in style, detail, and narrative technique, but also in theology and

Christology. As a result of their research, one can now speak not simply of Jesus, but of Matthew's Jesus, Mark's Jesus, Luke's Jesus, and John's Jesus.[1]

Imitating the example of New Testament scholars, I have chosen as my focus not Wilfrid, but *Stephen's* Wilfrid.[2] Such an approach differs markedly from the traditional approach of most historians of the early Middle Ages who have typically combed this saint's Life and others for factual information about the saint and his or her cult. Some will doubtless have wished that more energy had been spent in uncovering the Wilfrid of history and assessing his historical significance. Such a task, however, must await historians who are confident that their historical reconstruction and assessment of a saint is finally truer or more objective than the hagiographer's.[3] While a number of historians have already asked the larger question of what Wilfrid meant to the development of the English church and nation, few have asked in any detailed way the more modest question of what he meant to Stephen. This study addresses this latter question, based as it is on the conviction that Stephen's portrait of Wilfrid is as legitimate an object for historical study and analysis as the figure of Wilfrid himself.

This book's ultimate goal is to illuminate the theological convictions that undergird Stephen's *Life*. Its separate chapters have been arranged with that goal in mind. Chapter one begins with a general discussion of the nature and function of hagiography and then attempts to understand Stephen's *Life* in light of that discussion. Chapters two and three analyze the *Life* in terms both of its structure and of its typological characterization of Wilfrid as a martyr-like figure on the one hand and a fatherly mentor, or *pius pater*, on

---

[1] Of the many books that attempt to discern the distinctiveness of a given evangelist's portrait of Jesus and Jesus' life, *Mark's Story of Jesus* by Werner Kelber stands out for its clarity and conciseness. For a list and a survey of other works in this vein, see the first five chapters of Moore. (See *Works Cited* for complete information on works cited in this study.)

[2] Stephen's portrayal of Wilfrid is chronologically first. Other early portrayals include one by Bede (EH 5.19) and one by Alcuin (*Poem*, lines 577-645 in Godman 48-55). For recent accounts of Bede's portrayal of Wilfrid, see Isenberg 18-58 and Goffart 235-328, esp. 307-328.

[3] For an excellent comparison of the assumptions that govern the work of the modern empirical biographer, on the one hand, and the medieval hagiographer on the other, see Heffernan 38-71.

the other. Chapter four, the chapter that will be of greatest interest to most historians, attempts to trace the origins of Stephen's understanding of Wilfrid back to Wilfrid's own self-understanding as the latter was forged during Wilfrid's first pilgrimage to Rome and Lyon in the 650s.

Chapter five concludes the book by contrasting Stephen's portrayal of Wilfrid with the anonymous Lindisfarne monk's earlier portrayal of Cuthbert. That comparison brings the distinctiveness of Stephen's vision of Wilfrid's sanctity into bolder relief. By showing just how much was at stake theologically in Stephen's portrayal, chapter five calls into question some assumptions traditionally made by theologians and historians. Over against the theologians, it hopes to demonstrate that the Dark Ages had a deep interest in theological issues. Whereas theologians typically expect such issues to be addressed in a discursive or propositional form, recent Gospel research has shown that theological or religious convictions can be expressed with equal or greater power in narrative form. Just as the New Testament evangelist's narrative expresses a compelling religious vision, so too may the hagiographer's.[4] The author hopes that recognition of this fact will lead theologians to take hagiography more seriously as a source for historical theology than they previously have done.

Over against the historians, this book hopes to show that the study of Christianity in early Anglo-Saxon England can entail a good deal more than an investigation into ecclesiastical and dynastic politics. A good deal of energy has been expended over the years in debating, for example, whether or not Bede was pro- or anti-Wilfrid. The usual answers to that question, however different they might be, tend to be grounded in the assumption that the most suitable explanation is a political one--one that takes into account who Bede's friends and enemies were, which of those friends Wilfrid offended, and which he supported. Thus, one might argue, on the one hand, that because Bede sympathized deeply with the Irish party of Northumbrian Christians, he therefore disliked Wilfrid, who treated that party with

---

[4] Although the theological convictions of most Saints' Lives have gone unnoticed, one important exception is Athanasius' *Life of Antony*. Athanasius' wider reputation as an anti-Arian theological apologist doubtless encouraged scholars like Gregg and Groh to mine this *Life* for its theological content (Gregg and Groh 131-153).

contempt. Or, one might argue, on the other, that because Bede had such close relations with Acca of Hexham, Wilfrid's protégé, Bede probably liked and respected Wilfrid. Such answers are helpful, as far as they go, but they rarely seem to go much farther than considering the question in terms of any category other than that of sheer cronyism. While this study does not wish to dismiss the importance of considering such personal and political relations, it takes seriously the possibility that these relations themselves may have been forged out of yet more fundamental religious convictions about what it means to live humanly and faithfully within God's creation and under God's judgment. Thus, instead of collapsing religion into politics, this study assumes that political loyalties and antipathies may be expressions of a deeply held religious faith. Such an assumption may itself be perceived as an article of faith, and so it is. As such, it has the status of a mathematical axiom which admits neither of proof nor of disconfirmation. Because every work of scholarship must proceed on the basis of some such axioms, I make no apologies for this one, and state it explicitly at the outset.

The time between the writing of this book and its publication did not allow me to take as full account as I would have liked of several important books that came to my attention during that time. They include Thomas Heffernan's *Sacred Biography: Saints and their Biographers in the Middle Ages* and Nicholas Howe's *Migration and Mythmaking in Anglo-Saxon England*. Although in some ways quite different, these two books both encourage the reading of early medieval narratives not merely for the "historical facts" which these narratives contain, but for the mythic elements which they express. This way of approaching such narratives is congenial to my own approach to Stephen's *Life*.

Besides these two works, two others that pertain more specifically to Wilfrid and Cuthbert have appeared recently. The first, Walter Goffart's *The Narrators of Barbarian History*, shows how Bede's *Ecclesiastical History* was written in part to counter Stephen's interpretation of late seventh-century Northumbrian Christianity as Stephen put it forth in his *Life of Wilfrid*.[5] The

---

[5] See esp. pp. 307-324. Goffart's attention to Bede's reaction against Stephen's *Life* complements the attention given in this study, especially in chapter five, to Stephen's earlier reaction against the Lindisfarne anonymous' *Life of St. Cuthbert*.

second is the collection of papers given at the 1987 Cuthbert conference at the University of Durham under the title *St. Cuthbert: His Cult and His Community to A.D. 1200*, edited by Gerald Bonner, David Rollason, and Clare Stancliffe. Of the many fine papers in this volume, Benedicta Ward's stands out for its sensitive and warmly appreciative reading of Bede's *Prose Life of St. Cuthbert*. What she has done for Bede's Cuthbert, this book tries to do for Stephen's Wilfrid.

During the last ten years in which I have been thinking about Wilfrid and Stephen's *Life*, I have incurred debts to so many loyal friends and hospitable strangers that only a fraction of them can be named here. Generous funding for research in Britain came both from the United States-United Kingdom Educational Commission, which administered a Fulbright Grant from 1981 to 1983, and from Davidson College, which funded summer research time in England in 1986 and 1987. Because medievalists can never take all of the books that they need home with them, libraries become their second homes. I am therefore thankful for the hospitality and kind assistance offered me by librarians at Regenstein Library (University of Chicago), Palace Green Library (University of Durham), the Institute of Historical Research (University of London), the British Library, and Little Library (Davidson College).

Dr. Gabriele Isenberg kindly sent me a copy of her 1978 doctoral dissertation, *Die Würdigung Wilfrieds von York in der Historia Ecclesiastica gentis Anglorum Bedas und der Vita Wilfridi des Eddius*. This fine study, one of few to focus upon the theological and literary aspects of the earliest Wilfrid biographies, deserves far more attention and praise among English-speaking scholars than it has received. Having discovered it after writing the bulk of this study, I was happy, and humbled, to find that many of Dr. Isenberg's conclusions corroborated my own.

Three friendly colleagues--Peter Kaufman, Karl Plank, and Janet Summers--read this manuscript with a kindly critical eye at various stages of completion. The watchful eyes of Ron Foley, Pam Kelley, and Virginia Hall proofread the typescript.

Consideration of Stephen's portrayal of Wilfrid as fatherly mentor often put me in mind of my own mentors without whose wisdom, patience, and support this book could not have been written. They include Bernard

McGinn, Jerald Brauer, Robert Grant, Gerald Bonner, Patout Burns, Doug Petersen, Bob Johnston, and of course, my father, Olen Foley. Of these, a special word of thanks goes to Gerald Bonner, whose immense erudition and kindhearted constancy have aided me over the years in more ways than I can say.

The memory of a first mentor, as of a first love, can remain so vivid that its power to bless or curse one's life can be felt for a long time. The greatest blessing of my academic life is to have been introduced to the study of theology by the late John Bunyan Spencer of Kalamazoo College. This book is dedicated to his memory.

CHAPTER ONE

STEPHEN'S *LIFE OF BISHOP WILFRID*, HISTORY OR HAGIOGRAPHY?

In about 715, a man who identified himself as "Stephen the priest" sat down to write what some believe to be the first substantial piece of historical literature written by an Englishman.1 His labors brought forth a saint's Life of Wilfrid of York (d. 709), the colorful and controversial Northumbrian bishop and abbot who, since the Reformation, has earned great notoriety for attempting to establish the customs and authority of the Church of Rome as the norm for the Church in Anglo-Saxon England.

As any good student of hagiography knows, the historical value of medieval Lives of saints must be regarded with suspicion. Reports of the miraculous within them are so fantastic and so frequent that even the most credulous minds will refuse to accept them as documentary evidence of real historical events. The *Anonymous Life of St. Cuthbert* well exemplifies an early English saint's Life of the kind just described. Written in Northumbria at the end of the seventh century, it abounds in miracle stories and takes

---

1 The author's reference to himself as the priest Stephen (= *Stephani presbiteri*) occurs in the LW Praefatio. On the significance of the LW as historical literature, see Colgrave, "Earliest Lives" 57 and LW₂ ix (Introduction). In an insightful article, D. P. Kirby argues that the present version of the work to which I am referring--the priest Stephen's *Life of Wilfrid*--may not have been completed until the decade of the 730s, perhaps even after Bede completed the *Ecclesiastical History*. Kirby admits, however, that an earlier version of it was completed sometime between Wilfrid's death in 710 and the death of the Abbess Aelfflaed in 715 ("Bede" 107).

pains to portray the sanctity of the bishop Cuthbert largely in terms of his wonder-working powers.

By contrast Stephen's *Life of Wilfrid*, written less than twenty years after the *Anonymous Life of St. Cuthbert*, contains comparatively few incidents which modern historians would dismiss out of hand as incredible.2 It only occasionally depicts Wilfrid as a wonder-worker; its lengthy narrative, unlike that of so many other saints' Lives, adheres to a connected and strictly chronological narrative; and its attention to particular names, places and details--whether or not they are reported accurately--gives at least a greater impression of historicity than do some of the other earliest English saints' Lives.

Because Stephen's *Life of Wilfrid* conforms more closely than the other earliest English saints' Lives to our modern sense of what historical writing is, medieval historians have found it to be especially helpful in their attempt to reconstruct the social and political history of early Anglo-Saxon Northumbria and its church. In general they have regarded it as a richer mine for historical research than, for example, the earliest prose Lives of Cuthbert. Yet precisely because the *Life of Wilfrid* conforms more closely to the modern sense of an "historical" document, it has come under fire for historical inaccuracies (e.g., Poole 59-62). Few if any historians have ever criticized the *Anonymous Life of St. Cuthbert* on these grounds. To its author modern historians will impute purely hagiographical intentions and will therefore not judge him according to the canons of modern historical research. At the same time, however, they will impute to the priest Stephen a greater historical aim and will judge him harshly in accordance with those same canons.

This book has no concern either to attack or to defend the so-called "historical veracity" of Stephen's *Life of Wilfrid*. It has even less concern to

---

2 Although R. L. Poole believes that the author of the *Life of Wilfrid* greatly stretched the truth in order to suit his own apologetical ends, few would question that the life is at least written more in the style of modern, continuous, narrative biography than, for example, the *Anonymous Life of St. Cuthbert*. Although by modern standards, Stephen may be judged to be writing bad history, what he writes nevertheless seems to fall more easily into the category of historical writing than do such early English saints' lives as the lives of Cuthbert, Felix's *Life of St. Guthlac*, and *The Earliest Life of Gregory the Great*.

attack or defend Wilfrid's character. Since the Reformation, the figure of Wilfrid has been subject to scathing abuse from Protestants and fawning praise from Catholics and Anglo-Catholics.3 The lively debates that the controversial Wilfrid has sparked over the years--both in ecclesiastical and scholarly circles--seem to have grown more out of the desire of opposing factions to bolster their own modern theological and political convictions than out of any authentic concern to understand Wilfrid as Stephen or even Wilfrid did.

The Nature of Religious Convictions and Their Expression in Hagiographical Narrative

This study will mine Stephen's *Life of Wilfrid* for historical data of a different sort than has usually been sought. It has little or no concern to extract from Stephen's narrative new social, political, or even ecclesiastical information about early Christian Northumbria, but wishes rather to uncover certain religious convictions that Stephen's work presupposes and that inform its every page. A secondary and more modest aim will be to explore the extent to which Stephen's convictions, as expressed in his *Life*, may reflect Wilfrid's own and how Wilfrid would have come by them. Chapters two, three, and five of this book will pursue the former aim; chapter four, the latter.

In using the phrase *religious convictions*, the word *religious* is meant to connote more than simply Christian; and *convictions* more than simply propositions of belief that are expressed in creedal or doctrinal formulations. To uncover the Christian dogmas that Stephen's text takes for granted would

---

3 Perhaps the most extreme examples of Protestant abuse come from two eighteenth-century historians, John Inett and Thomas Carte. Inett was inclined to think that "the Hardships that fell upon Wilfrid were conducted by the Divine Justice" (*Origines* 1:90), while Thomas Carte excoriated Wilfrid as one who, being "very fond of himself," exhibited "a certain haughtiness of mind" which, though resulting from his "natural disposition," was made worse by the "maxims he had imbibed at Rome" (*A General History* 1:235). At the other end of the spectrum, the Anglo-Catholic Frederick William Faber praised Wilfrid for his "Catholic instinct," which made him "look Romeward," and for his "true Yorkshire cheerfulness." For a fuller discussion on what historians since the Reformation have said about Wilfrid, see Foley, "St. Wilfrid of York as *Pius Pater*" 8-40 and Farmer, "Saint Wilfrid" 35.

be a relatively easy task. They would have included, for example, the Christological and Trinitarian formulations of Nicaea, Chalcedon, and the other ecumenical councils of the church. The harder task is to articulate the universal and existential relevance of Stephen's story for human living more generally, and not merely for an orthodox Christian audience. To complete successfully such a task, a more comprehensive and less parochial understanding of the phrase *religious convictions* is needed.

The late theologian Paul Tillich provides a useful definition of religion which can be employed for the purpose of coming to just such a better understanding of what a religious conviction is.4 According to Tillich, the word *religious* really points to the uniquely human state of being grasped by an ultimate concern (*Theology of Culture* 7-8). To be so grasped points to a realm in which human beings experience a sacred, mysterious, and numinous power not subject to their manipulation. On the contrary, they experience their ultimate concern as having power over and energizing both themselves and the cosmos; it undergirds their being and the being of all that is. As ultimate concern, one's object of religious devotion eclipses all other preliminary concerns. A man may be concerned about avoiding conflict, but the fact that he is willing to go to war reveals that the simple avoidance of conflict does not constitute his ultimate concern. A woman may be concerned to perpetuate her life, but her willingness to die in order to save her child's life shows that the mere preservation of her biological self is not her ultimate concern. Human beings experience that which ultimately concerns them as that unconditional good without which every other good seems valueless. As such, they are unable to be indifferent to it or dispassionate about it. As their ultimate good, it evokes their ultimate loyalty, so that if necessary, all other goods--perhaps even oneself--will readily be sacrificed on its behalf. The word *conviction*, like the word *religious*, also has to do with basic allegiances. It describes a fundamental attitude or orientation, not derived from discursive thought, on which a

---

4 Tillich's definition of religion provides only one helpful way to think more broadly about what a religious conviction might be. There are doubtless other helpful ways and the author makes no claims for either the exclusivity or superiority of Tillich's definition.

person bases all other opinions and attitudes. Convictions are neither ideas nor propositions, but the foundational bedrock of both. What cultural anthropologist Victor Turner says about *root paradigms* holds equally true for convictions: "They go beyond the cognitive, and even the moral, to the existential domain....They reach down to the irreducible life stances of individuals, passing beneath conscious prehension to a fiduciary hold on what the individual senses to be axiomatic values, matters literally of life and death" (*Process* 148).5 Convictions have a self-evident and unconditional quality about them. Whereas in common parlance a man is said to hold convictions, in fact, just the opposite is the case: a man's convictions hold him. One can tinker with one's ideas--change them, modify them, reject them. Convictions do not admit of such easy manipulation.

Convictions also motivate and orient human behavior. By offering a compelling vision of what is ultimately good and by exciting passion for it, convictions cause men and women to live and behave with some consistency. A woman, for example, will not betray what her convictions tell her to be goodness itself, nor will she befriend what they tell her to be evil. Convictions, therefore, determine the ends for which human beings act.

A person's convictions do not all operate on the same level. Some are deeply embedded within the self, others less so. Those nearer the surface can be abandoned with less pain and radical reorientation than those at the core. A man may, for example, be motivated by a conviction which values the importance of self-sacrifice on one level and yet, when offered the option of sacrificial death or renunciation of the self-sacrificing conviction, he decides for the latter. Such an example would show that beneath his conviction about self-sacrifice lies a deeper conviction about the ultimate meaningfulness of perpetuating his own organic existence, without which, to him, his other acts of self-sacrifice hold no meaning. By qualifying the term *conviction* with the adjective *religious*, one expressly signifies those root convictions that abide at the deepest levels of the human self.

---

5 This discussion is also indebted to Daniel Patte's insights on the nature of convictions (*Paul's Faith* 10-27; D. Patte and A. Patte, *Structural Exegesis* 101-103).

Internal vs. External History

Unlike other studies of Stephen's *Life of Bishop Wilfrid* that concern themselves chiefly with external matters of fact and information, this one will focus upon the religious convictions that undergird Stephen's narrative. The author will devote little time to the historians' more traditional historical questions which might be asked about Wilfrid, questions such as: "What role did dynastic infighting play in the evolution of Wilfrid's career?" "How large was Wilfrid's monastic empire?" and "Was Bede's attitude toward Wilfrid friendly or hostile?"6 Such a statement does not mean that this work has no concern for historians. On the contrary, it intends historians as its primary audience. The history with which it will be concerned, however, is not history in the conventional sense of reportage, of reconstructing events as they really happened, or of explaining the mechanics and evolution of certain social and political institutions. It is history, rather, in the sense of recovering how events and the persons within them were remembered, valued, and interpreted by the authors who originally preserved their memory. Our particular concern in this regard will be with the priest Stephen as author and with how his *Life* remembers, values, and interprets the figure of Wilfrid. In order to do history in this sense, one must do more than simply mine Stephen's *Life of Wilfrid* for the nuggets of information which lie on or close to the text's surface. One must work to expose the text's convictions both about the person of Wilfrid and about those issues of ultimacy--of ultimate good and ultimate evil--which properly constitute the religious realm.

In order to clarify the kind of history which will concern us here, it may be useful to distinguish between what American theologian H. Richard Niebuhr has called internal and external history (42-54). According to Niebuhr, the modern post-Enlightenment study of history belongs to the category of external history. As such, it takes the impersonal method of modern science as its paradigm. The scientific historian, as historian, writes

---

6 The first question is addressed by Kirby in "Northumbria"; the second by Roper in "Wilfrid's Landholdings"; the third by a host of historians, whom Goffart has helpfully catalogued (254, n. 98).

from the viewpoint of the detached observer rather than the active participant. She places great value on empirical observation and does not care (at least not as *qua* historian) about how her investigations turn out. Just as the scientist *qua* scientist remains unmoved when he discovers a new and deadly form of cancer, so does the historian *qua* historian read with cool objectivity eyewitness accounts of the Nazi holocaust. To be sure, as human beings who live, who will die, and who hate the necessity of death, that same historian and scientist may care deeply about those death-dealing phenomena which they have observed. They may even write deeply moving and personal accounts of the existential meaning that their investigations have had for them. As scientific observers, however, they will attempt to suspend their passionate and sometimes violent feelings in the hope that their scientific objectivity will yield a good which their raw passion will not.

Whereas modern secular historians concern themselves almost wholly with what Niebuhr calls external history, early Christian historians concerned themselves with internal history. When the four evangelists wrote their stories of Jesus, when Athanasius wrote his *Life of Antony*, when Eusebius wrote his history of the early church, and when the earliest English hagiographers like Bede, Stephen, and Felix wrote their respective *Lives*, all did so from the point of view of those who, as valuing selves rather than impartial scientists, participated in and therefore cared passionately about the history within which they lived and about which they wrote.

Written from an involved rather than a detached viewpoint, such documents of internal history have as their aim something other than an impersonal presentation of facts and of hypotheses which issue from them. Thus, the authors of the Gospels do not seek simply to impart biographical information about the historical person Jesus of Nazareth. They seek rather to remember him and to celebrate him as the Christ and, by so doing, to invite their readers to do likewise.7 Similarly, early church historians such as

---

7 This insight has been fundamental to New Testament scholarship in the twentieth century. See Dahl; Johnson 11-29; and Käsemann, "Is the Gospel Objective?" 58-62. Students of medieval hagiography might draw fruitfully from this fund of scholarship, applying its insights about the relationships among Jesus, the early church, and the Gospel genre more generally to the relationships among saint, saint's cult, and saint's *Life*.

Eusebius and Bede have as their aim not merely to highlight the historical factors which led to the victory of Christianity over paganism in their respective geographical regions, but to present that victory as the express result of God's providential activity, to call their readers to recognize that activity within their own histories, and to live accordingly. Finally, the medieval hagiographer's primary aim is neither to narrate curious and idiosyncratic details about the saint's Life nor to communicate truths otherwise unknown about the saint's historical milieu. It is rather to present the saint as an authentic type of Christ through whom God calls sinful humanity to repentance, conversion, and Christ-like imitation. As New Testament theologian Rudolf Bultmann might say of an evangelist's depiction of Jesus, so might one also say of the hagiographer's depiction of the saint: it calls the reader not to intellectual assent of this or that historical detail, but to an existential recognition of and obedience to the power of God as it is manifest in the hearing or reading of the saint's *Life*.

Like all other saints' Lives, Stephen's narrative begins and ends with the conviction that the power of God was manifest in Wilfrid in a special way. It aims not to report to its audience the bare facts of Wilfrid's life, but to convey the providential meaning of that life to those who will view it with the eyes of faith. This earliest *Life of Wilfrid* cannot thus claim a detached observer as its author. Nor can it claim a detached audience. Stephen writes in the preface that the work was commissioned by Bishop Acca and Abbot Tatberht, both ardent disciples and chief heirs of Wilfrid's spiritual legacy.8 Stephen states, moreover, that in addition to the commissioning of these two, the whole community prodded him to finish his task. That "whole community" may refer to Wilfrid's entire monastic *familia*, though the entire work seems to address more specifically the interests of Wilfrid's monastic *familia* at Ripon.9 The Ripon *familia* doubtless cherished the memory of

---

8 Acca was Bishop of Hexham, a see which Wilfrid established and for which he built his most magnificent church (LW ch. 22). According to Stephen, Wilfrid handpicked Tatberht, his kinsman, to succeed him as abbot at Ripon, the mother house of Wilfrid's monastic *familia* [LW ch. 62(63)].

9 Kirby, "Bede" 110-111; Isenberg 95-102.

Wilfrid in a special way, for Ripon was the first-born of all his monastic *familiae*, the resting place of his remains, and thus the central shrine of his early cult. There more than anywhere else the monastic *familia* daily witnessed poignant reminders of Wilfrid's life and death, weekly observed Thursday (Wilfrid's death-day) "as a feast as though it were a Sunday," and annually celebrated his earthly life as well as the continued presence of his spirit among them on the anniversary of his death (LW 64(65)).

Stephen's *Life*, therefore, represents far more than simply his own point of view. Its very existence presupposes an entire community's active attempt to remember Wilfrid's life as well as their common conviction that this particular life conveys a sense of life's ultimate meaning and goodness to all who are open to it. As a product of a community's internal history, Stephen's *Life* cares less about getting the facts straight than with conveying the common meaning and significance which that life held for Wilfrid's spiritual *familia*. If constrained by the orders of Acca and Tatberht, Stephen is no less constrained by the larger community's common conviction about Wilfrid's sanctity. All would have agreed with Stephen's conviction that "to know him is the perfect way to virtue."10

Hagiography's Theological Dimensions

New Testament scholars have long realized that the evangelists did not write their separate accounts of Jesus' life and ministry merely to impart dispassionate knowledge about him. They wrote rather to proclaim in their own ways that Jesus is Lord and to exhort their audiences to respond in kind. As has been just noted, the medieval hagiographer and the New Testament evangelist share common ends. Both write from the standpoint of internal

---

10 LW praefatio: *"Est siquidem perfecta via ad virtutem illum scire."* In saying this, Stephen is copying verbatim from the prologue of the *Anonymous Life of St. Cuthbert*. The latter is itself compiled from the Victorius of Aquitaine's *Cursus Paschalis* ch. 1, Athanasius' *Life of Antony*, and Sulpicius' *Life of St. Martin*. For full reference, see LW₁ 193, n. 1. The fact that this statement is not original to Stephen does not mean that it represents imperfectly both his and the Ripon community's own views. On the contrary, his borrowing from the *Anonymous* author underscores the parallel between the esteem in which Wilfrid was held by his community and the esteem in which Cuthbert was held by his.

history. Although the hagiographer certainly recognizes the evangelists' claims for the special status of Jesus (Jesus and only Jesus is the Christ), the hagiographer's narrative usually expresses the conviction that the saint that it celebrates is a near perfect type of Christ, that the saint's life story shows forth the image of Christ in an especially telling way. While hagiographers have not always agreed about what it means to show forth the image of Christ, they nevertheless have attempted separately to articulate their respective views about that image's essence. Moreover, they have attempted to answer for their various audiences the Christological question that the figure of Jesus asks of all who would be his disciples: "But who do you say that I am?" (Mt. 16:15). The hagiographer usually answers that question not explicitly, but implicitly, by choosing to depict the saint in a particular way. For some, the image of Christ is best represented in the type of the persecuted prophet or apostle; for others, in the ascetic; and for still others, in the wonder-worker. Even if the hagiographer depicts the saint as being a combination of these and other types, the reader can nevertheless almost always note with profit which types of sanctity the author chooses to emphasize and which are hardly mentioned at all. As I shall argue in chapter five, at stake in this depiction are not only the hagiographer's parochial prejudices and penultimate loyalties, but his or her deepest convictions about ultimacy--what is ultimately good and what is ultimately evil in human life. In this way the hagiographer's discussion of the saint and the meaning of the saint's life grows out of something more than just the desire to promote or justify the saint's cult. That discussion and the saint himself or herself become a vehicle for talking about the reality of God, the plight of sinful humanity, and possibilities for redemption.

Saints as Signs

Whereas a modern biography's success depends largely upon the author's ability to convey a sense of his or her subject's unapproachable uniqueness, the medieval saint's life presupposes just the opposite. The saint is held up as an object for our esteem because of his or her twofold typicality: the saint typifies both the Christ who reigns in glory and the human Christ who experienced temptation, abandonment, and death. Although the vigor with which the hagiographer depicts the saint's superhuman qualities may obscure the latter aspect, the very fact that the life is narrated to provide its audience with an example for imitation--as the prefaces of many *Lives* explicitly state--reveals the hagiographer's conviction that what the saint has become through God's grace remains possible for anyone who hears and responds to God's call.

As a type, the saint's life becomes less important for what it was factually, than for what it signifies about the reality of God. To ask what it was without due concern for its theological significance, significance to a human self passionately concerned with life's ultimate meaning and value, is to ask the question of external history. Belonging as it does to internal history, early Christian biography radically subordinates such factual questions to those about meaning and significance. For this reason the hagiographer's tendency to relate the incredulous and the miraculous still baffles the modern mind, concerned as it is with empirical fact. Modern readers must realize, however, that the hagiographer's tendency to stretch the empirical truth grows not out of an intrinsically deceitful or gullible nature, but rather out of the conviction that what moderns call "empirical reality" reflects, but does not include that which concerns human beings ultimately. To put it more theologically, the earthly kingdom shows forth signs of God, but does not finally contain God.

Few have articulated better than St. Augustine this distinction between corporeal signs on the one hand and the God whom they signify on the other. By so doing he formally gave medieval men and women a hermeneutical principle which enabled them to discern and interpret the hidden meaning of the entire created order, including Scripture, nature, history, and--most importantly for our present purposes--the saint's life. In *On Christian Doctrine*, Augustine explains this distinction in terms of things "to be enjoyed" and "things to be used":

> Some things are to be enjoyed, others to be used, and there are others which are to be enjoyed and used. Those things which are to be enjoyed make us blessed. Those things which are to be used help and, as it were, sustain us as we move toward blessedness in order that we may gain and cling to those things

> which make us blessed....To enjoy something is to cling to it with love for its own sake. To use something, however, is to employ it in obtaining that which you love, provided that it is worthy of love. (1.3.3, 1.4.4)

For the hagiographer to have an interest in the saint simply for the saint's own sake would correlate to what Augustine calls "enjoyment." The hagiographer's depiction of the saint would thus become a thing to be enjoyed in its own right by those who either read or hear the *Life*. Augustine would condemn any such enjoyment of the *Life* or the saint depicted therein. By enjoying creation's lesser goods, including any human life or its written record, in themselves (or for their own sakes), the human person forfeits enjoyment of the highest good, which is God. Since God alone can bring true joy to the human heart, God alone is to be enjoyed (OCD 1.5).

The tangible and empirical realities of this life, though not to be enjoyed in themselves, are not to be despised, but rather *used* to guide human life back to that from which it is estranged--God's abundant goodness:

> Thus in this mortal life, wandering from God, if we wish to return to our native country where we can be blessed, we should use this world and not enjoy it, so that the *invisible things* of God *being understood by the things that are made* may be seen, that is, so that by means of corporeal and temporal things we may comprehend the eternal and spiritual.11 (1.4.4)

Following this logic, the reader begins to see from Augustine's perspective the proper way to approach the saint and the saint's *Life*, as well as the proper end toward which the hagiographer directs his or her narrative art. As things which belong to the created order, both the saint and the saint's *Life* belong to the category of "things to be used"--to be used, that is, as vehicles which carry the person who encounters them back toward enjoyment of God. The saint, therefore, distinguishes himself or herself in

---

11 Italics added to indicate Augustine's allusion to Rom. 1.20: "For the invisible things of him [God]...are clearly seen, being understood by the things that are made" (Douay-Rheims Version). Because the wording of the Latin version of this Romans passage differs somewhat in sense from the Greek upon which the RSV is based, the Douay-Rheims translation of this passage is cited here. The Douay-Rheims Bible is a somewhat literal translation of the Latin Vulgate Bible which, in this Romans passage at least, closely approximates Augustine's Latin text of Scripture.

the extraordinary way that he or she directs an erring and errant humanity
back to its proper end:

> Thus, the proud man or the proud angel places his enjoyment
> in himself and rejoices that others place their hopes in him
> also. But the holy man and the holy angel refresh us with what
> they have received, and only with what they have received,
> either for themselves or for us, and even though we are
> wearied and desire to rest and to remain with them, they urge
> us onward when we have been refreshed toward Him in whose
> enjoyment we may both be blessed. (1.33.36)

Heeding Augustine's counsel, the medieval hagiographer wanted to
distract the audience's attention from anything about the saint which did not
serve the larger end of movement toward God. If the hagiographer seems to
gloss over the seamier side of the saint's personality or to say little about his
or her personal idiosyncrasies, one need not conclude that the hagiographer
has an uncritical attitude toward the saint or has set about to deceive the
credulous. To do otherwise, namely, to dwell on these idiosyncrasies for
their own sake, would only serve to direct the audience's interest to the saint
as an interesting character in his or her own right. Once that is done, the
saint's value as saint ceases. For as Augustine notes, saints are so called only
so long as they point beyond their own peculiar accomplishments toward
what God has accomplished in and through them (1.33.36).

The Nature and Function of Stephen's *Life of Wilfrid*

Although Stephen may not have depended directly upon Augustine's
theory of signs, his understanding of the significance of Wilfrid's life surely
lies closer to Augustine's view than to a modern-day biographer's. If Stephen
thus chooses to overlook or embellish certain details of Wilfrid's life, he does
so not necessarily to deceive his audience, but--as Augustine might put it--to
move them toward blessedness in enjoyment of God. His aim was not to tell
his readers what a modern might call the "naked" or the "whole" truth about
Wilfrid. It was to tell a truth that would edify. In this respect, Stephen's
selective representation of Wilfrid closely resembles the evangelists' selective
representation of Jesus, Eusebius' selective representation of Origen or

Constantine, or the anonymous Lindisfarne monk's selective representation of Cuthbert.

Like these other early Christian biographers, Stephen wrote within the context of a particular community and reflects that community's particular perspective. Unlike modern biographers, Stephen did not see his association with Wilfrid's monastic *familia* at Ripon as one which distorted his view about Wilfrid or made him biased to such an extent that he could not tell the edifying truth about his old abbot as he and others in the Ripon community had witnessed it. Objectivity must have hardly been an issue for him since he never meant merely to document certain cold and clinical details about Wilfrid's career, but wanted rather to tell Wilfrid's story in a way that reflected his community's conviction that this man pointed to the reality of God. Because of this concern for ultimacy, Stephen's purpose has the status of a religious concern.

Stephen also has more idiosyncratic concerns, but he does not try to hide them. He thus stands in marked contrast to modern biographers who attempt to transcend the biases and viewpoints of their own sociohistorical communities, thinking that by so doing they somehow gain an objectively truer picture of the subject in question. Modern people almost always see the more authoritative viewpoint as being the more detached one, the one least informed by the author's subjective feelings of affection or loathing for the subject.

Yet just because a saint's *Life* points beyond worldly concerns at one level does not preclude the presence of those concerns at another. Being human, Stephen has penultimate concerns as well as an ultimate concern. This being so, he not only wishes to point his reader toward God, he also hopes to justify Wilfrid against his detractors. Such justification of Wilfrid doubtless contains an element of self-justification and community hubris. In his preface, Stephen indicates that Wilfrid's earthly reputation has suffered attack from enemies and that he means to defend it. He writes:

> I implore the readers to trust the things said here, *leaving behind the thousand envious pricks of the ancient enemy and contemplating instead what eloquence has thundered forth. For courage always has its rivals in the open air:* "And lightning

strikes the mountain tops first." (LW Praefatio--author's translation and emphasis)

Although Stephen has copied much of his preface verbatim from the *Anonymous Life of St. Cuthbert*, the italicized words in the above quotation are his own additions.12 These additions reveal Stephen's conviction that defending Wilfrid's memory involved him in a cosmic as well as a human conflict. For the text makes it clear that the prime instigator of Wilfrid's character assassination is none other than Satan himself. To defend Wilfrid is thus to fight Satan, and to fight Satan is to labor against the chief obstacle over which humanity must stumble on its way toward God. Whereas modern historians have tended to impute little more than a purely this-worldly partisanship to Stephen for defending Wilfrid, Stephen himself saw that defense as somehow important to what concerns human beings ultimately. For him the quarrel between Wilfrid and Wilfrid's detractors functions as a type for the cosmic combat between God and Satan, ultimate Good and ultimate Evil.

One can only guess the identity of those whom Stephen saw as Wilfrid's maligners. Stephen's *Life* offers no dearth of possible candidates. Perhaps they included certain descendants, kinsmen, and friends of Wilfrid's several royal enemies; or staunch supporters of Archbishop Theodore and his programs for ecclesiastical reform; or certain monastic communities that remained strongly attached to such Celtic traditions as were transmitted to Northumbria through Iona and Lindisfarne.13 Whoever they were, they doubtless denied Stephen's claim that Wilfrid was a holy man. Embedded in their rejection of Wilfrid must lie their own deep-rooted convictions about sanctity, about God, and about how God's activity properly reveals itself in the lives of God's chosen. The debate about Wilfrid thus shows itself to be, at its deepest level, a theological debate.

Of all those detractors of Wilfrid whom Stephen's *Life* may intend to counter, special interest will be paid here to those whose devotion to St.

---

12 Stephen borrows the final quote about lightning striking the mountain tops from Horace via the prologue to Jerome's *Liber Hebraicorum Quaestionum in Genesim* (PL 23.935B).

13 On the enmity that the Lindisfarne community may have had for Wilfrid, see Colgrave, *Two Lives* 357.

Cuthbert's cult made them unwilling to view Wilfrid as a holy man at all. Although Wilfrid survived Cuthbert by about twenty-two years, both men were born in Northumbria in about 634. They are thus exact contemporaries, yet apparently quite different in spirit. In Cuthbert one finds the perfect representative of a holy man in the Hiberno-Saxon tradition of Iona and Lindisfarne. Devotees of his early cult remembered him for his rigorous asceticism, his strong eremitic impulse, his powers as a wonder-worker and seer, and his intimate relations with the natural world. Although he served as bishop of Lindisfarne for a brief time, his reputation for sanctity rested more securely on personal charisma than on his specifically episcopal deeds. In 698, the monks of the Lindisfarne community exhumed the body of their beloved bishop from its resting place in the Lindisfarne church and found his remains incorrupt.14 This event helped to spread Cuthbert's cult and within a year or so an anonymous monk of Lindisfarne had completed writing the first *Life of St. Cuthbert*. This *Life* has strong claim to being the earliest work of hagiography written in Anglo-Saxon England.

Though never mentioned in Stephen's narrative, the imposing figure of St. Cuthbert seems to cast a decisive background shadow out of which Stephen hopes to bring the memory of Wilfrid into more prominent relief. Stephen makes no secret of his knowledge of the *Anonymous Life*. As seen already, the preface to Stephen's *Life* is copied almost verbatim from the *Anonymous Life*'s preface. In addition, Stephen draws his stylized description of Wilfrid's episcopal virtues in chapter 11 from the *Anonymous Life* (4.1).

Despite these considerable borrowings, Stephen's literary depiction of Wilfrid differs markedly from the anonymous' depiction of Cuthbert. These differences highlight each author's own understanding of that which distinguishes his respective hero as a type of Christ or a holy man. The anonymous monk of Lindisfarne casts Cuthbert in the Christlike mold of the ideal monk, a type well known to the Christian hagiographical tradition through such works as Athanasius' *Life of Antony* (ca. 357) and Sulpicius' *Life of St. Martin* (ca. 394-397). At the heart of this tradition lies the conviction

---

14 LCA 4.14.

that the most perfect imitation of Christ consists of a lifetime of daily, ascetic self-denial. Although Stephen shows himself to be in no way hostile to the Antonian, ascetic type which dominates the Cuthbert *Life*, he nevertheless chooses to depict Wilfrid as belonging to the tradition of several other Christ-types: the apostle, the prophet, the confessor, and the martyr. For Stephen, each of these types is intimately related to the others by virtue of their single, shared experience: the patient suffering of persecution at human hands. The types of persecuted apostle and prophet dominate Stephen's representation of Wilfrid.15 Over against the type of the monk, they belong to a more primitive understanding of Christian sanctity, one that goes back to the first two Christian centuries and accords well with the canonical and apocryphal Acts of the Apostles, the early martyrs' *Acta*, and the theology of Tertullian. Why Stephen wished to depict Wilfrid, the great Northumbrian abbot and establisher of the Benedictine *Rule* in Northumbria, more as martyr than monk should mystify readers of the *Life* more than it apparently has. As I shall argue in chapter four, Stephen's depiction may have foundations in Wilfrid's own understanding of himself and his mission, a self-understanding shaped in part during six influential years of his youth when he was on pilgrimage to Rome.

In conjunction with the types that undergo persecution, Stephen characterizes Wilfrid in accordance with a second type: the *pius pater* or devoted father. In this role, Wilfrid acts as mentor and protector to every class of society--monks, the poor, and even kings. The notion of spiritual fatherhood can be traced to a very early stratum of Christian tradition. That notion, however, underwent considerable change during the era of the later Latin fathers. A purely spiritualized understanding of a pastor's and bishop's role that characterized the early tradition gave way to a more all-embracing one from the fourth century onwards. Bishops like Ambrose of Milan, Augustine of Hippo, Desiderius of Cahors, and Eucherius of Lyon exercised their episcopal authority more vigorously than had their predecessors. In so doing they transformed existing understandings of the pastor's fatherly role

---

15 On Wilfrid as apostle, see Isenberg 64-71; as prophet, see Mayr-Harting 139-141.

by tacitly appealing both to fatherly models, drawn from aristocratic Roman family life, and to leadership models, drawn from Roman political life.

This combination of the persecuted apostle and prophet types with the *pius pater* type gives Stephen's characterization of Wilfrid its unique stamp. In Stephen's mind and heart, Wilfrid's perfect embodiment of these two Christ types makes him equal in status not only to the brother apostles Peter and Andrew, as he states at the end of his work, but to Cuthbert, whom he never mentions. As I shall argue in the following chapters, Stephen's decision to model Wilfrid after these types instead of after the ideal of the ascetic wonder-worker has significant theological consequences which issue from his deepest convictions about both Wilfrid and the ultimate questions of human existence: about ultimate goodness, where it resides, how it should be loved, whether it can be befriended; and about evil, where it impoverishes life most fatally, how it is to be avoided, whether it can be defeated.

These deeply human questions surely concerned Wilfrid himself, though we can have no direct access to how he would have answered them. Like New Testament scholars who have learned so well that the Christ of faith is not identical to the Jesus of history, students of hagiography who examine Wilfrid must likewise realize that the Wilfrid who lived, evangelized, and taught before his death in 709 is not the idealized Wilfrid whom Stephen, the Ripon *familia*, and the rest of the early Wilfrid cult commemorated and venerated after the saint's death.

Yet certain continuities between historical reality and hagiographical memory do exist. The frequency of these continuities largely depends upon the hagiographer's temporal and intellectual proximity to the saint about whom he is writing. With respect to temporal proximity one would expect, for example, that the continuities between the historical Wilfrid and his early cult's memory of him are greater than those between the historical Jesus and the early church's memory. The written memory of Jesus' life and passion begins with the Gospel of Mark, written in about 70 C.E. by someone who almost assuredly was *not* an eyewitness of the events he describes. By contrast, Stephen probably finished the *Life of Wilfrid* between 710 and 715, at most only five or six years after Wilfrid's death.16

Moreover, unlike the author of Mark's Gospel, Stephen had known Wilfrid personally as his abbot and had firsthand access to others who were his most intimate companions, most notably Acca and Tatberht. For this reason also, there should be a greater intellectual proximity between Wilfrid and Stephen than can be expected from most hagiographers and their subjects. Contrast this to the case of Jesus and the evangelists, for example. New Testament scholarship has shown that there was often a great chasm between Jesus' own understanding of his life and mission and the understanding that the early church had of the same. Over the years, the early church came to see Jesus more and more as the fulfillment of certain Old Testament types, such as Abraham, Adam, and Jonah. This tendency to interpret Jesus' experience as well as its own in terms of types illustrate the early church's creative genius. As part of the early Christian legacy to the medieval church, this typological way of interpreting a human life was doubtless shared by Wilfrid and his community. Wilfrid would surely have been unable to interpret his life's trials and tribulations as he did without reference to those types which Scripture and tradition had bequeathed to him. His community, having suffered along with him, must have interpreted their own experience in the same terms.

For these reasons, the student of Wilfrid (and here, for once, I mean the Wilfrid of external history) has a comparatively hopeful prospect for reconstructing Wilfrid's self-understanding--though perhaps not the external events of his life--from Stephen's narrative. A reconstruction that depended on several more independent accounts from members of Wilfrid's inner circle at Hexham or in Mercia would make historians more comfortable, but no such accounts exist except those that Bede mentions in his *Ecclesiastical History*.17 Despite Bede's help in reconstructing certain aspects of Wilfrid's

---

16 LW ch. 59 indicates that Stephen was writing while the Abbess Aelfflaed was still living. Bede reports in HE 3.24 that Aelfflaed died in 715. The *Life of Wilfrid* must, therefore, have been written sometime between 710 and 715.

career, aspects about which Stephen says little or nothing, Bede offers little help in reconstructing the religious convictions of Wilfrid and his *familia*. For although he writes about Wilfrid with much admiration, and assigns him a crucial role in God's plan for bringing the gospel to the English people, he does not understand him from an insider's perspective as Stephen does. Bede's own internal history binds him more closely to the story of his own monastic *familia* at Wearmouth-Jarrow and to its telling and interpretation of the mighty acts that God has wrought in order to convert the English. In addition, his authorship of a *Prose Life* and a *Metrical Life* of Cuthbert shows that he was more easily able to adopt the internal history of the Lindisfarne community than that of Ripon as his own.

Like it or not, we must rely almost entirely upon Stephen for the kind of information about Wilfrid's piety and self-understanding that we seek. That conclusion need not disappoint the student eager to know about Wilfrid. For in Stephen's story the reader will encounter one of the richest texts that early English hagiography has to offer. Rich in biblical associations, typological imagery, and theological vision, the *Life of Wilfrid* will yield up to the thoughtful student fresh insights and discoveries with each new reading. Even if its readers were to conclude after long study that its portrait of Wilfrid bears no relation to Wilfrid's own self-understanding, they would have to concede that the time required with the text to draw that conclusion was profitably spent. Like any good saint's Life, Stephen's *Life of Wilfrid* will send its readers back to the biblical text again and again, inviting them to participate in a vital discussion about sanctity and salvation history and, as part of that process, reacquainting them with that biblical "cloud of witnesses" whose lives--in Stephen's mind--Wilfrid so faithfully imitated (LW ch. 35; cf. Heb. 12.1).

---

17 Most notable in this respect is the information about Wilfrid that Bede received from his close friend, Bishop Acca of Hexham, who was also Wilfrid's devoted disciple. See, for example, EH 2.13 and 4.14.

CHAPTER TWO

WILFRID AS TYPE OF CHRIST (I)--
PERSECUTED APOSTLE, PROPHET, AND CONFESSOR

Since the second half of the nineteenth century, historians of Anglo-Saxon England have often emphasized its predominantly Germanic character. The great English constitutional historian William Stubbs typified this point of view:

> With the exception of ecclesiastical influence, no foreign interference that was not German in origin was admitted at all [into Anglo-Saxon England]. Language, law, custom, and religion preserve their original conformation and colouring. The German element is the paternal element in our system, natural and political. (11)

Despite Stubbs's warning that this Germanic influence did not fully apply in the ecclesiastical realm, historians have sometimes tried to find Germanic influence even there. The relationship between the lord and his thegns, for example, is sometimes seen as the prototype for the relationship between the Anglo-Saxon abbot and his monks; the heathen heroic preoccupation with the treasure-hoard is imagined to be behind every reference in the original sources to ecclesiastical decoration and episcopal finances; and the struggle of the Germanic epic hero with primeval monsters is seen to prefigure Anglo-Saxon hagiographical accounts of the holy man's struggle with demons.

Such quests for the Germanic influence within early English Christianity, though sometimes justified, can be taken too far, and in

22

Wilfrid's case they often have been. For example, several historians have paralleled Stephen's account of the aged Wilfrid distributing his treasury with the old warrior Beowulf surveying his hoard.1 Another implies that the devotion of Wilfrid's monks to him was rooted no less in a Germanic *comitatus*-style loyalty than in the Benedictine *Rule*'s call for unquestioning obedience to the abbot (Albertson 19-22; 145, n. 7; 152, n. 113). A noted historian of Anglo-Saxon England recently summarized such understandings of Wilfrid best when he said, "Wilfrid was a great saint, of colossal spiritual energy and commitment, but his life retains much of the flavour of the Germanic warlord."2

In the attempt to use Stephen's *Life of Wilfrid* as an indicator for the Germanic or heroic nature of early Anglo-Saxon culture, the *Life*'s status as a work of early Christian literature has been all but lost. Examined so long as a source for external history by English and medieval historians, Stephen's work now needs to examined as internal history by theologians, literary critics, and patristics scholars.

However much Wilfrid's life reminds today's Anglo-Saxon historian of Beowulf or some other Germanic warrior-aristocrat, it chiefly reminded Stephen of the lives of the apostles, prophets, and patriarchs. Moreover, each of those lives, along with Wilfrid's, reminded him of the life of Christ, and *vice versa*. Stephen's many explicit and implied references to these biblical types are the prisms through which he beholds and interprets Wilfrid's life. They constitute one of the most striking features--and the most wearisome--of Stephen's hagiographical style.

The Typological Imagination in Paul and in Early Christianity

To understand the dynamics of early Christian narrative and exegesis, one must examine how believers in the early church interpreted their own

1 Cf. R. H. Hodgkin 346; Thomas Hodgkin 213; Mayr-Harting 228; Wormald 54-55; Campbell 174. For similar accounts of Wilfrid's likeness to a Germanic warrior-hero, see Albertson 158, n. 127.

2 Wormald in Campbell, *The Anglo-Saxons* 83.

experience in terms of these old biblical types. The apostle Paul himself uses the word *type* (1 Cor. 10.6; Rom. 5.14) to denote a pattern or example which he sees as occurring both in the Hebrew Scriptures, in the experience of Jesus the Christ, in his own experience, and within the experience of the early church.3 For example, in 1 Corinthians 10.1-5, Paul discerns a common pattern within the historic experience of Israel, on the one hand, and the early church, on the other. He implicitly likens the Hebrews' passing through the Red Sea (Ex 14.22) to the Christian baptism ceremony, and he likens the Hebrews' experience of being fed in the wilderness (Num. 20.7-11) to the early Christian eucharistic meal. Here Israel is a type for the early church in two senses. First, Israel's experience of deliverance from Pharoah is a type of the church's experience of deliverance from sin and death. As types, both experiences are regarded by Paul as typical of the way in which God intervenes in human experience to redeem it. Secondly, Israel's behavior is a type for the church's behavior. That is, the particular ways that Israel acted as God's chosen people offer examples, both bad and good, from which the church should learn and either imitate or avoid. In this particular case, Paul offers up Israel's "rising up to dance" (Num. 20.7), "indulging in immorality" (v. 8), "putting the Lord to the test" (v. 9), and "grumbling" (v. 10) as negative examples which should warn the church against idolatry. In the first sense, the type is descriptive; in the second, prescriptive. That is, the first type describes how Israel's experience in the wilderness is typical of what Christians have already experienced in baptism and eucharist. The second type prescribes future behavior for Christians based on what the Israelites have already done. Moreover, the type's prescriptive sense derives its power from the descriptive: it is especially because both the Old Israel and the New Israel have been called and redeemed by God (i.e., descriptive sense) that they should avoid idolatrous behaviors (i.e., prescriptive sense).

Although Paul only uses the word *type* in a few places, a typological understanding of himself, the church, and Christ permeates his writing. Not only does the experience of the Old Israel typologically prefigure the New, so

---

3 This entire section on Paul's typological interpretation of scripture, Christ, and his own experience relies heavily on Patte *Paul's Faith*, 131-154, 190-231.

does the experience of Abraham's being justified by faith prefigure the Christian's justification (Rom. 4.1-25; Gal. 3.1-18), as does Christ's experience of dying on the cross and rising from the dead prefigure the believer's experience in baptism (Rom. 6.1-14). Examples like these could be enumerated again and again from Paul's writings. Before citing too many examples, however, let us first explore in greater detail how all these types typify the various experiences of God's chosen.

In Romans 8.30 Paul provides a key to the general typological pattern at work in each of the examples mentioned above as well as in all the others that figure prominently in his framework of salvation history. Speaking of the stages by which God redeems humanity, Paul writes: "And those whom he [God] predestined he also called; and those whom he called he also justified; and those whom he justified he also glorified" (Rom. 8.30). For Paul as for other early Christian authors, this process of predestination, call, justification, and glorification typifies the way in which the believer comes to experience God's saving power.

Since Paul neither dwells upon predestination nor clarifies what he means by it, one can only guess that it simply highlights for him the fact that God, and no human person, has provided the initiative in forging the relationship between God and God's elect. One would infer rightly from this that neither Abraham, Moses, Old Israel, the prophets, Christ, Paul, nor the Church chose themselves. Rather they were chosen before they ever had the chance to prove themselves in any way worthy.

The second stage, the call, involves the actual setting apart of the believer within the believer's own experience. The call typically involves both an initial revelation of God's power and God's promise of a continuing, saving relationship with the believer. In addition, the call implicitly invites the believer to trust in God's ability and intention to fulfill what has been promised, even during situations in which the demonic powers of sin and death seem to have claimed a victory which makes fulfillment of the divine promise impossible. In the case of Abraham, God's call came through the "promise to Abraham and his descendants that they should inherit the world" and through the invitation of Abraham to believe that the promise's fulfillment would "not come through the righteousness of the law, but through faith" (Rom. 4.13). As Abraham's offspring, Christ experienced God's call through the promise to Abraham and Abraham's seed as it had been made known through Scripture (Gal. 3.16). In other words, just as God's spoken promise functioned as the call to Abraham, so did the preservation of that promise within the written word of Scripture function as the call to Christ (Patte 213). Moreover, like Abraham and Christ, Paul and the early Christians experience a call from God: Paul through Christ (Gal. 1.11-12), and the Christians at Thessalonica through the power of the Holy Spirit as manifested in Paul's preaching of the gospel (1 Th. 1.5).

The revelation of God's power does not, however, destroy finally the power of sin and death in the believer's experience. On the contrary, the believer experiences that evil power in such an acute fashion that God's promise of blessing at moments of crisis seems to have been nullified by it. Yet for Paul, God graciously chooses such seemingly hopeless situations as the occasion to manifest the divine power of salvation. Evidence of that power can be seen in the believer's resurrection-like experiences. Such experiences include, for example, the ongoing experiences of faith and joy which occur in the very midst of the suffering which death, sickness, persecution and other death-like experiences bring.[4] These experiences are but several instances of the primary miracle of *justification*, which occurs through faith. For Paul, justification is a resurrection-like experience. For in both justification and resurrection, God is experienced as intervening to save the believer from a death-dealing power. To speak of justification presupposes, in some sense, that the believer is not wholly just, that he or she is a sinner. Abraham's status as sinner is--according to a first-century Pharisaic, Torah-centered perspective--owing to his uncircumcision (Rom. 4.11). Even Christ is said to have been "in the likeness of sinful flesh" (Rom. 8.3), "made to be sin" (2 Cor. 5.21), and to have "become a curse for us" (Gal. 3.13). As such, Abraham and Christ become types for all of humanity--both Jew (Rom. 2.1-11) and Gentile (Rom. 1.18-32).

---

4 What Paul Tillich refers to as "the power of non-being" indicates something of what we mean here by "death-like experiences." For Tillich, as for Paul, faith and the courage that accompanies it overcomes the destructive power of non-being. See, for example, *Dynamics of Faith* 16-22.

Yet despite their status as sinners, these types abandon neither their hope, which is grounded in their initial experience of God's revelation in power to them, nor their faith that God is able to do what God initially promised. Nor are they disappointed. For in the hopeless situation of being one hundred years old, Abraham and Sarah had a son, Isaac, in accordance with God's promise (Rom. 4.13-25); in the hopeless situation of crucifixion, Christ was raised from the dead; in the hopeless situation of persecution, the church experiences an outpouring of joy (1 Th. 1.6). Justification, therefore, overcomes the believer's hopeless situation and is experienced by the believer as miracle (Patte 221).

In the process of justification, God works continually to bring about the defeat of evil powers which threaten to destroy human life. These defeats, however, are all only partial. For example, the Thessalonians' experience of joy in the midst of persecutions does not save them permanently from those forces which harass them: they are still subject to further persecution, evil, sin, and death. The fourth and final stage of *glorification* constitutes God's final and decisive victory over the powers of sin and evil, so that the believer who has been glorified is no longer subject to them. One might say that glorification is the final work of justification. In this regard, Christ's justification through his resurrection from the dead represents a unique manifestation of God's justifying power. For in resurrection, the Christ "who became sin" is not only justified, but glorified. As such, he becomes a type, and a source of hope, for those who have experienced God's call and justification, but who still anticipate the hopeless situation of bodily death and sin. For Paul, Christ alone has been glorified. And yet, as type, he anticipates the glorification of those who are his "fellow heirs" (Rom. 8.17), namely, those who imitate him in the twofold sense of 1) experiencing the power of God as he experienced it and 2) behaving as Christ behaved.

Stephen's Depiction of Wilfrid as a Type of Christ

The early medieval hagiographer operated as much out of a typological mode of understanding both Scripture and contemporary history as Paul did, perhaps more so. Just as Paul had designated Christ and Abraham as types of right relationship with God for early Christians, so did those early Christians themselves also become types of that right relationship for later generations of Christians. These later generations came to look upon the apostles and the early Christian martyrs as men and women who, like Abraham and Christ, also faced hopeless situations of persecution and, with persecution, God's justifying and redeeming activity which manifested itself in their superhuman courage and joy. Along with Christ, therefore, the apostles and martyrs also became examples for imitation in the twofold sense described above. Later, early Christian monks and hermits, who sought to imitate the example of Christ and the martyrs, themselves became types for the imitation of others.

With the rise of the cult of the martyrs, the hagiographer began to think of the departed saint as already glorified, just as Christ is. The accounts of miracles of healing and deliverance occurring at the saint's tomb declare that the saint who was subject to sin and death in this life is now immune from it.5 The saint now reigns in power with God and, as one of God's elect, administers the life-sustaining power of God at his or her shrine. The miracles at the saint's tomb function as signs that the saint does not simply lie dead in the ground, but is already actively working to do God's work, to defeat the powers of sin and death (Brown, *Cult* 106-127). Whereas for Paul, resurrection and glorification had been experienced only by Christ, though promised to his saints, later hagiographers believed that that promise was already being fulfilled.

Following the exegetical method of Paul, the Church Fathers, and other early medieval hagiographers, Stephen interpreted Wilfrid's life in typological terms. What uniquely distinguishes his narrative, however, is the extent to which he makes explicit Wilfrid's conformity to each of the four stages of redemption. Like the authors of the canonical gospels, Stephen is not content simply to offer us a scene here, a miracle there, from his subject's life. He chooses rather to narrate its full course. In this respect, his *Life of*

5 The immunity of the saints from the power of sin and death is mentioned, among other places, in Augustine, *On Rebuke and Grace* ch. 33.

Wilfrid differs significantly from the two prose Lives of Cuthbert between which it was sandwiched in time.6 The Cuthbert Lives offer little sense of the dramatic unity which comes from the narration of a life as a continuous sequence of events. They attempt rather to convey Cuthbert's sanctity through isolated, usually discontinuous, vignettes and miracle stories. Indeed, such indications as they do provide of sequential happenings within Cuthbert's life are scarcely essential to their theological and literary potency. By contrast, Stephen's *Life* carefully weaves each scene and vignette into the larger narrative framework so that the entire *Life* says much more than simply the sum of its parts.

The Literary Structure of Stephen's *Life of Wilfrid*

A careful reading of Stephen's *Life* with an eye to its plot and literary structure will reveal several distinct phases. The first presents Wilfrid's call and preparation as bishop (chs. 1-23); the second relates the persecutions and trials he experienced as bishop and the vindication he won from Rome (chs. 24-55); the third, a kind of denouement, depicts Wilfrid both at the end of his life and after his death as finally triumphant over his foes (chs. 56-68). The *Life*'s threefold structure thus mirrors the Pauline scheme of redemption as it is expressed in Romans 8.29-30. The first section tells the story of predestination and call; the second, of justification, and the third, of glorification. Those who doubt whether Stephen had this particular scheme explicitly in mind should note that he cites these verses from Romans in his first chapter, almost as if he were laying out a roadmap for what lay ahead. Although he may have taken his cue here from the *Anonymous Life of Cuthbert* 1.3, where the same Pauline verses are only partially cited, he nevertheless makes greater use of the salvation scheme that it contains. Indeed, an outline of Stephen's entire work reveals just how closely the narrative structure mirrors the fourfold process articulated in Romans 8.29-

---

6 I am referring here to the *Life* of the anonymous monk of Lindisfarne (ca. 700), and Bede's *Prose Life* (ca. 721). For a further discussion of these lives and their dates, see Colgrave, *Two Lives* 11-16.

30 (see Appendix I). The following consideration of that outline will help the reader to understand the *Life*'s entire framework as well as its constituent parts.

Predestined (Chapter 1)

At the opening of chapter one, Stephen writes:

> So, with God helping and by Wilfrid's holy merits, I shall begin to write the life of the blessed Bishop Wilfrid, whom the Lord, in the words of the excellent teacher, *foreknew, predestined, called, justified and glorified*.[7] For from the womb of his own deeply pious mother, a sign demonstrated that he had been sanctified by God, just as Jeremiah heard a word from the Lord, saying, *"Before I formed you in the belly, I knew you; and before you came out of the womb I sanctified you; and I made you as a prophet among the nations."*[8] (author's translation)

Stephen goes on to relate how at Wilfrid's birth, a great fire rose to the heavens from the house in which the saint was born. That fire is implicitly identified with the Holy Spirit which, through Wilfrid, would soon manifest itself to nearly all the churches of Britain.[9] Putting his typological imagination to work, Stephen interprets the sign of the flames by juxtaposing Wilfrid's prenatal experience of sanctification with the prophet Jeremiah's. What does this sign mean? It means that Wilfrid, like Jeremiah, was foreknown and predestined by God to be "a prophet among the nations."

Called (Chapters 2-23)

In the following chapters, Stephen gradually unfolds the story of Wilfrid's divine call as an apostle to the English (chs. 2-4), Wilfrid's preparation for that call in Rome (ch. 5), the threats posed to its fulfillment in Lyon, the overcoming of that threat by God's intervention (chs. 4, 6), and finally the initial spectacular success of Wilfrid's apostolic work in

---

7 Rom. 8.29-30.

8 Jer. 1.5.

9 Stephen here articulates a principle that was stated in the previous chapter, namely, that saint Wilfrid, like all saints, functions as a sign that points beyond himself to the Holy Spirit which is at work in and through him. See the section "Saints as Signs" in chapter one, above.

Northumbria (chs. 7-23). This last part, the longest subsection within the entire calling section, confirms for the reader the conviction articulated in earlier chapters that Wilfrid had experienced and heeded an authentic divine call.

In order to stress the divine nature of Wilfrid's call, Stephen contrasts early on his hero's motivation for leaving home (ch. 2) with Wilfrid's later motivation for visiting Rome (ch. 3). The decision to leave home is depicted as Wilfrid's own, resulting directly from bad relations with his cruel stepmother. It results in his admission to the monastic community at Lindisfarne where he waits upon the nobleman Cudda. By contrast, Wilfrid's desire at Lindisfarne to visit the see of Peter in Rome is said to have "arisen within the heart" of Wilfrid at the suggestion of the Holy Spirit.10 As the narrative unfolds, the reader will learn more about the special nature of Wilfrid's call. When he informs Cudda and Queen Eanflaed of his wish to see Rome, these two send him on his way via Canterbury and Lyon (LW chs. 3-4). At Lyon in Gaul, Wilfrid's devotion to his divine call is tested when Lyon's Archbishop Dalfinus tempts him to abandon his mission, offering Wilfrid a "large part of Gaul" to govern and his niece to wed.11 Although one must read Dalfinus's offer as a gesture of affection, Stephen's allusions to Satan's temptations of Christ--especially the temptation to rule the kingdoms of the world (Lk. 4.5-8; Mt. 4.810)--can hardly be missed. Wilfrid resists this temptation, and in so doing, finally reveals the specific nature of his divine commission. He says:

> To the Lord belong my vows which I shall fulfill, leaving kin and my father's house as Abraham did, so that I might visit the Apostolic See and learn the rules of ecclesiastical discipline in order to increase the service of God among our people. (LW ch. 4)

---

10 LW ch. 3: "Deinde post circulum annorum, suggerente Spiritu sancto, apellare et videre sedem apostoli Petri...in cor adolescentis supradicti ascendit...."

11 Both the AsA and the *fasti* of the church of Lyon record the name of the bishop who reigned during Wilfrid's visit as Annemundus. Both Stephen and Bede, however, give his name as Dalfinus. Colgrave suggests that Dalfinus was the name of Archbishop Annemundus' brother, the count of Lyon, and that Stephen and Bede confused the brother's names (LW₂ 153). Eugen Ewig believes that the name Dalfinus was the archbishop's first or second name and one by which an intimate like Wilfrid would have called him ("Milo" 210, n. 111).

Just as Paul's special commission is to the Gentiles, Wilfrid's is to the English in order that they might serve God by learning and observing *the rules of ecclesiastical discipline* which are taught most purely in Rome.12 Stephen here implies that the English cannot properly serve God unless they also properly observe ecclesiastical discipline.

With this brief temptation scene, Stephen announces two themes which will appear repeatedly in his narrative. The first and more central theme concerns the absolute necessity of observing proper ecclesiastical discipline. As Stephen will assert again and again, such observance constitutes the cornerstone of faithful commitment to God and upon it rests the integrity of the church in general, and of the English churches in particular. The second has to do with Gaul's status as a place of trial and temptation (LW chs. 6, 13, 27, 33, 56). As the geographical midpoint on the route between England and Rome, a route which Wilfrid will traverse three times in his life, Gaul is assigned a mythological significance as the place where evil powers are at work to destroy the link which Wilfrid has been called specially to forge between the English churches and the apostolic see.

In chapter five, where Wilfrid arrives in Rome, Stephen again emphasizes the central role that the establishing of ecclesiastical discipline will play in defining Wilfrid's calling. There, the reader is told, Boniface the archdeacon taught Wilfrid the Easter rule and "many other rules of ecclesiastical discipline."13 With this knowledge of canon law firmly in his grasp, Wilfrid's training is complete. Stephen can now bring the call narrative to its climax by describing how the "pope of blessed memory" laid his hand on young Wilfrid's head and blessed him, a ritual act which recalls the imposition of hands upon Stephen (Acts 6.6) and Paul (Acts 13.3) before they began their public ministry (Isenberg 59-60).

In chapter six, Wilfrid returns from Rome to Lyon and remains there for a three-year stint, at the end of which his mettle is again tested. In a curious act of double-mindedness, Archbishop Dalfinus shaves Wilfrid's head

---

12 LW ch. 4: "ecclesiasticae disciplinae regulas didicerim."

13 LW ch. 5: "et alias multas ecclesiasticae disciplinae regulas."

in the form of the Petrine tonsure, thus initiating him into the monastic life, while secretly desiring to have Wilfrid as his heir. Just as the pope put his hand on Wilfrid's head, so does Dalfinus. This ritual action, performed a second time within the space of several lines, highlights what Stephen sees as God's special purpose: to make Wilfrid an evangelist in the mold of such biblical heros as Paul and Stephen, the first Christian martyr (cf. Acts 13.3; 6.6). Reinforcing the claim that Wilfrid received a special call from God to serve as apostle to the English, Stephen goes on to say that Dalfinus' wish to keep Wilfrid as heir contradicts God's purposes, for "God was providing for our nation something better for [the English] race" than what Dalfinus intended (ch. 6).

In what is interpreted as an act of divine intervention, providentially designed to sever Wilfrid's ties to Lyon, Dalfinus suffers martyrdom under the Frankish queen Balthild. Besides being the spur which drives Wilfrid back to England and his mission, the martyrdom of Dalfinus in Stephen's portrayal provides an appropriate setting for highlighting Wilfrid's faithfulness and obedience to his divine calling. Reminiscent of the young Origen, whom Eusebius depicts as so zealous for martyrdom, Wilfrid eagerly accompanies Dalfinus to the place of execution, hoping to die with him.14 Typologically, this situation of grave danger for Wilfrid parallels such biblical scenes as Abraham's sacrifice of Isaac or Jesus' crucifixion. In each case, the man of God is confronted with an apparently hopeless situation which seems to render fulfillment of a previous divine promise and call impossible: if Isaac dies, how can Abraham fulfill his divine call to become the father of many nations? (Gen. 17.4); if Jesus dies, what happens to the promise that he will redeem Israel? (cf. Lk. 24.21); and if Wilfrid suffers martyrdom with Dalfinus, how will the English, being ignorant of the rules of ecclesiastical discipline, "grow in the service of God" (LW ch. 4)? Can the Holy Spirit's prompting of Wilfrid to learn those rules in Rome and to transmit them to the English have been in vain (LW ch. 3)?

Yet just as God intervenes to fulfill the promise made to such biblical types as Abraham and Christ, so does God here intervene to redeem the

---

14 Eusebius, *Ecclesiastical History* 6.2.3.

promises made to Wilfrid. Having already been "despoiled and prepared for martyrdom," Wilfrid is recognized as an Englishman and his life is thus spared. By virtue of this ordeal, he has earned the status of "confessor," and forthwith returns triumphantly to England in order to begin his mission.

In these first six chapters Stephen foreshadows the dramatic tensions and motifs that will dominate the rest of the narrative. We have already noted the theme of Gaul as the place of trial. In addition, Queen Balthild's persecution of Dalfinus and the other Gallic bishops points ahead to the Northumbrian kings' persecution of Wilfrid. Ready for martyrdom, the young Wilfrid is described in chapter six as "despoiled" (*spoliatus*), a word which Stephen will use repeatedly in connection with Wilfrid's degradation at the hands of the Northumbrian kings.15 Foreshadowed also in Wilfrid's first trip to Rome are his later two trips in which he will appeal to the apostolic authority against the decisions which the Northumbrian kings rendered against him. Although the young Wilfrid has no case to prosecute on his first trip, Stephen cleverly uses the word *appello*, in the sense of "to move toward," to describe Wilfrid's movement toward Rome at the opening of chapter three. *Appello*, however, may also mean more specifically "to make an appeal" or "to implore" in precisely the manner that Wilfrid would make an appeal to Rome on his next two visits there. In fact, Stephen will use the word later in its more specific sense in connection with Wilfrid's appeal process (chs. 24, 47).

Arriving back in England, Wilfrid's spectacular successes as abbot (ch. 8), priest (ch. 9), teacher of ecclesiastical discipline (ch. 10), and bishop (chs. 11-23; esp. ch. 21) all serve to confirm his divine calling as Rome's apostle to the English. Chapters 7-23, which narrate this period between Wilfrid's return from Rome and his expulsion from the Northumbrian see by King Ecgfrith, comprise a logical literary unit. From Stephen's point of view, this period is the golden age of Wilfrid's life and career. He thus takes great pains to stress his conviction that Wilfrid's good fortune during these years results from God's graciousness and unchanging purpose for him. God had not abandoned him in "the days of his poverty" when his stepmother and

---

15 LW chs. 25, 34, 39, 43 (twice), 47, 53.

Queen Balthild had persecuted him, and the wonders and miracles he now performs attest to that fact.16 Having demonstrated God's faithfulness to Wilfrid during Wilfrid's past afflictions, Stephen lays the groundwork which enables the reader to regard Wilfrid's afflictions in later chapters not as a sign of divine displeasure, but as the kind of test that God has always sent to the elect (cf. LW ch. 35).

Justified (Chapters 24-55)

After narrating Wilfrid's call to be both a bishop and an evangelist who has special responsibility for teaching the rules of ecclesiastical discipline to the English, Stephen begins the "justification" section of his *Life* (chs. 24-55). In it Wilfrid undergoes a thrice-repeated cycle, each occurrence of which consists of two parts: persecution at the hands of a Northumbrian king and intervention by God through the authority of the apostolic see in Rome. The first cycle (chs. 24-33) begins with King Ecgfrith's and Archbishop Theodore's persecution of Wilfrid and includes Wilfrid's expulsion from Northumbria (chs. 24-28), his subsequent appeal to Rome (chs. 29-30), and his exoneration in Rome by Pope Agatho and his synod (chs. 31-33).

The second cycle (chs. 34-44) begins immediately after the completion of the first. Ecgfrith again plays the role of the persecuting king. He despises the pope's decrees and imprisons Wilfrid (ch. 34), during which time miracles occur to confirm Wilfrid's status as an apostle and prophet of God (chs. 35-39). Following imprisonment, Wilfrid works as an exiled missionary among the Mercians, South Saxons, and West Saxons (chs. 40-42). The divine intervention in this second cycle occurs through Archbishop Theodore of Canterbury, Wilfrid's former persecutor. Theodore offers Wilfrid not only reconciliation--with himself, Northumbria's King Aldfrith, and Mercia's King

---

16 Colgrave has translated the enigmatic phrase "quid animo gerebat in pauperte" in LW chapter 8 as "what his [i.e., Wilfrid's] intention had been in the days of his poverty" (LW$_2$ 19). In a similar way he has translated "in angustiis suis" at the end of chapter 9 as "in the days of his poverty" (LW$_2$ 19). This latter phrase might be construed more generally as "in his difficult days," referring back to his difficult domestic situation (ch. 2) or to the danger he experienced in Lyon with Dalfinus (ch. 6). In this subsection (chs. 7-23), Wilfrid performs the only two miracles which Stephen reports as having occurred during Wilfrid's lifetime (chs. 18, 23).

Aethilred--but also the archiepiscopal see of Canterbury (ch. 43). In writing this dialogue between Theodore and Wilfrid, Stephen takes great pains to put words like "by the apostolic authority" or "by God and St. Peter" on the lips of both men, thus highlighting the role which Rome's apostolic authority plays as God's special agent of deliverance. Thus justified, Wilfrid returns triumphantly to Northumbria, his Northumbrian monasteries and his episcopal see at York having been restored (ch. 44).

The third and final cycle (chs. 45-55) of the justification section begins immediately after Wilfrid's reconciliation with Theodore. This time Aldfrith plays the role of the persecuting Northumbrian king who deprives the monastery at Ripon of its territories, its possessions, and its papally granted liberty, and who enforces certain of Archbishop Theodore's more offensive original decrees, though Stephen does not explicitly name which ones (ch. 45). In addition, King Aldfrith and certain of his bishops and abbots try to dupe Wilfrid into signing a document which would deprive him of his possessions and rights (chs. 46-47). During this final period of persecution, Wilfrid's enemies not only attack Wilfrid, they also refuse to communicate with any of his monastic or clerical *familia*, treating even the vessels from which they ate "as though polluted with filth" (ch. 49). Once again Wilfrid travels to Rome seeking divine deliverance which he receives "through the help of God and through Saint Peter"[17] by the agency of Pope John and an assembly of bishops and priests (chs. 50-55). Wilfrid is then sent home armed with relics and with a document from Pope John ordering Kings Aethilred and Aldfrith to attend a local synod convened by Archbishop Berhtwald in order to conclude the matter and to do Wilfrid justice.

Throughout the justification section, Wilfrid's persecutors regard him as a scandal--and not only Wilfrid, but his monks and priests as well (cf. ch. 49). Wilfrid thereby functions as an imitable type of the persecuted Christ for *his* spiritual children in the same way that Paul does for the Thessalonian church (1 Th. 1.6). Lifting up this theme of persecution, Stephen likens Wilfrid to the suffering servant in the book of Isaiah: Wilfrid is "a sheep led

---

17 LW ch. 53: "...Deo et sancto Petro principe apostolorum revelante et aperiente...", and later "soleque veritatis per Dei adiutorium et sanctum Petrum illuscente...."

to the slaughter" (LW ch. 36; Is. 53.7). Yet with their rich associational imagination, Stephen and Wilfrid's monastic *familia* would not have regarded Wilfrid as the only slaughtered sheep. As Benedictine monks who daily pored over and meditated upon Scripture, and who recited the Divine Psalter once a week, they would have remembered that in chapter eight of Romans Paul appeals to the image of the slaughtered sheep from Psalm 43.22 (not from Isaiah 53), and applies it to the entire community of believers.18 They would have also encountered the image of the slaughtered sheep in RB 7.38, where Benedict describes the fourth step of humility:

> The fourth step of humility is that in this obedience under difficult, unfavorable, or even unjust conditions, his heart quietly embraces suffering and endures it without weakening or seeking escape. . . . Another passage shows how the faithful must endure everything, even contradiction for the Lord's sake, saying in the person of those who suffer, "For your sake we are put to death continually; we are regarded as sheep marked for slaughter" [Rom. 8.36; Vg Ps. 43.22]. (RB 7.35-36a, 38)

Wilfrid himself thus becomes a type for the Benedictine monk climbing the ladder of humility.

Just as Wilfrid has become an offense to his enemies, so has the entire community (ch. 49). Like Christ, both have "become a curse" (Gal. 3.13); like an apostle, both have become as "the refuse of the world" to those who see with worldly eyes (1 Cor. 4.13). Indeed, Wilfrid's enemies are said to have ordered that any food blessed by one of Wilfrid's abbots or priests be regarded quite literally as refuse, and "thrown outside and cast away as if offered to idols" (ch. 49). Nevertheless, having become an offense to their enemies, Wilfrid and his *familia* continue to enjoy the miracle of justification whereby the persecuted are made by God to endure. Indeed, so crucial is this theme of justification amidst persecution to Stephen's narrative that he devotes about one-half of the entire *Life* to its development.

---

18 Vg Rom 8.36: "Sicut scriptum est: Quia propter te mortificamur tota die: Aestimati sumus sicut oves occisionis." Cf. Vg Ps. 43.22: "Aestimati sumus sicut oves occisionis"; Vg Is. 53.7: "Sicut ovis ad occisionem ducetur ...et non aperiet os suum"; and LW ch. 36: "quasi ovem ad occisionem qui non aperuit os suum." The RB prescribes recitation of the entire Psalter once a week (18.23).

Critics of Stephen's *Life* have objected, in effect, that the Wilfrid who is portrayed there has greater concern for self-justification than for divine justification.19 To be sure, Stephen's Wilfrid vigorously defends his rights, if not his righteousness, yet he always does so strictly in terms of the norms of canon law, and never in terms of God's absolute norms of justice. What Stephen hopes to establish, therefore, is not Wilfrid's angelic goodness, but the legitimacy of Wilfrid's divine calling as the teacher and upholder of Roman ecclesiastical discipline. If Wilfrid had simply resigned himself to his fate, he would have also resigned his divinely appointed role as protector of the canons among the English. Instead, he embraces that calling and the persecution which it entails, not trying to secure deliverance by his own wits, but waiting patiently for divine intervention.

Glorified (Chapters 56-68)

One of the most dramatic of such interventions marks the beginning of the *Life*'s final section on *glorification* (chs. 56-68). In chapter 56, Stephen tells how Wilfrid, passing through Gaul on his way back to England, was seized with an illness so severe that he had to be carried on a litter. His comrades, fully expecting him to die, convey him to the town of Meaux where he lies unconscious and without nourishment for four days and four nights. On the fifth day, the angel Michael appears to Wilfrid and tells him that because of the Virgin Mary's intercession he will recover, return safely to England, receive back his dearest possessions, and live four more years. Michael further advises the old bishop to build a church in honor of "St. Mary, mother of God and ever Virgin." After the angel departs, Wilfrid recovers miraculously and resumes his journey.

Angels and superhuman figures appear only twice in the entire *Life*. Besides the angel Michael's appearance here, a young man arrayed in white appears after Wilfrid's death when arsonists attack Wilfrid's monastery at Oundle [ch. 66(67)]. Since Stephen, unlike so many hagiographers, makes rare mention in his *Life* of supernatural and miraculous events, one ought to note that when he does, he may be trying to offer his audience a special

---

19 See, for example, Carte 235; R. H. Hodgkin 344; and Stenton 145.

signpost toward the correct interpretation of Wilfrid's life story. As eschatological figures, these angels point to events of eschatological significance within the life of Wilfrid's communities. Their irruption onto the scene marks a decisive turning point within Stephen's narrative. In the first instance, the archangel Michael's appearance marks the end of Wilfrid's persecutions and the beginning of his glorification. Recalling the angel's appearance to the shepherds in the Lukan birth narrative, Stephen writes, "Behold! an angel of the Lord in bright apparel appeared to our holy bishop."[20] In addition, Stephen has Michael say, "And this shall be a sign to you," and then prophesy Wilfrid's restoration. The angel in the Lukan birth narrative utters essentially the same formula when telling the shepherds how they will recognize the Christ child.[21]

This angelic appearance and Wilfrid's revivification at Meaux in chapter 56 marks the beginning of his glorification. From that point forward, both Wilfrid and his *familia* become invulnerable to the assaults of their persecutors. Returning to England with the papal documents, Wilfrid submits them first to King Aethilred of Mercia, who willingly consents to their terms, and to King Aldfrith of Northumbria, who does not. Because of his obstinacy, Aldfrith is struck down by the "divine vengeance" working through the "apostolic power" and dies. His successor Eadwulf pursues Wilfrid with equal vigor and threatens to kill any of the bishop's companions who remain in his kingdom. Far from doing Wilfrid or his *familia* any harm, Eadwulf himself is driven from the kingdom after only a two-month reign. Osred, son of Aldfrith, succeeds him and "is made an adopted son by our bishop" (ch. 59). At a synod at the river Nidd, Osred and the bishops who had excommunicated Wilfrid and his *familia* at last make their peace with him and communicate with him in the breaking of bread. Wilfrid receives back his two best monasteries, Ripon and Hexham, with all their revenues;

---

20 Cf. Vg Lk. 2.9: "Et *ecce angelus Domini* stetit iuxta illos, et claritas Dei circumfulsit illos" and LW ch. 56: "*ecce! angelus Domini in veste candida* sancto pontifici nostro apparuit." Another close biblical parallel to Stephen's narrative can be found in Vg Acts 10.30 when Cornelius describes the appearance of a man to him: "...et *ecce* vir stetit ante me *in veste candida*" (italics added).

21 Cf. LW ch. 56: "et hoc tibi erit signum"; and Vg Lk. 2.12: "Et hoc vobis signum."

exiles from his *familia* return; and all live together in peace until Wilfrid dies some four years later.

In these closing chapters, Stephen makes it clear that Wilfrid's long years of suffering and tribulation were not in vain. As a reward for so patiently enduring persecution, God at last transforms Wilfrid's weakness and vulnerability into strength and power after his death. In life, Wilfrid could not shield the members of his *familia* from the trials which beset them; in death, he becomes their greatest protector from would-be persecutors. Stephen interprets the *familia*'s experience of being thus safeguarded as a sign of Wilfrid's glorification. Having drawn upon imagery from Christ's birth to describe the beginning of Wilfrid's glorification at Meaux, Stephen now borrows imagery from Christ's resurrection to signify the perfection of Wilfrid's glorification after death. In chapter 67, when a group of noble exiles come to burn Wilfrid's monastery at Oundle, one of their number enters the house where the old bishop died and finds there a young man in white who stands holding a golden cross in his hand. Frightened by this vision, the marauder leaves and exhorts his companions to do the same, saying: "Let us depart from this place. Behold! an angel of the Lord is defending this house." The image of one who enters an enclosed space, sees a young angelic man in white, becomes afraid, and flees belongs also to the end of Mark's gospel where the two Marys and Salome come to Jesus' tomb, find a young man in a white robe, become afraid, and run away (Mk 16.1-8).22 Just as this episode in Mark's gospel signifies Jesus' resurrection, so does the corresponding episode in Stephen's *Life* signify Wilfrid's glorification. Imitating the spirit of the evangelists, Stephen expresses his community's conviction that Wilfrid, like Christ, does not lie dead in the grave, but lives on as that community's defender and protector. Just as the apostolic power once protected Wilfrid and struck down his enemies, so now does the glorified Wilfrid do the same for his communities. For this reason, Stephen declares that Wilfrid has been made equal to the brother apostles,

---

22 Cf. LW ch. 67(68): "hominem iuvenem stantem in albis"; and Mk 16.5: "iuvenem ...coopertum stola candida."

Peter and Andrew, both of whom are associated strongly with the apostolic
power of Rome [LW ch. 67(68)].

A Theology of Persecution and Glorification

As the preceding analysis of literary structure indicates, Stephen
depicts Wilfrid in accordance with Paul's typological understanding of Christ
and the Christian life. In his fourfold experience of divine election, Wilfrid is
shown as a true imitator of the Christlike pattern. But what, for Stephen, did
such imitation concretely entail? So numerous were the understandings of
Christlike imitation within the early medieval church that one must examine
more specifically which styles of Christlikeness Stephen saw Wilfrid as
embodying. Does he cast Wilfrid primarily in the mold of an apostle, a
prophet, an ascetic, a cenobite, a hermit, a pilgrim, a seer, a healer, or a
mystic? Or does he depict Wilfrid as a combination of two or more of these
traditional Christ types?

As a cursory reading of the *Life* will reveal, Stephen uses a
combination of these types to develop his portrait of Wilfrid. For example,
he depicts Wilfrid as healer (chs. 18, 23), ascetic (ch. 21), seer (ch. 24), and
pilgrim-exile (chs. 24-55). These types, however, do not dominate Stephen's
characterization of his hero. Whenever Stephen makes an explicit or implied
comparison between Wilfrid and another type of Christ, he almost always
refers to a biblical character, usually either a New Testament apostle or an
Old Testament prophet. Appendix II below shows that Stephen's favorite
apostles are Paul and Peter, with John and Andrew also receiving mention.
The more frequent references to Paul and Peter may derive from their close
associations with Rome or may simply reflect their more frequent mention
among the apostles in the New Testament. Among the prophets, Stephen
has no clear favorites. They include Elijah, Elisha, Moses, Samuel, David,
Daniel, and Ezekiel.23

---

23 That Stephen should present Wilfrid in the mold of an apostle and a prophet rather than
the ideal monk is, in some respects, curious. As the one who brought the Benedictine
observance to the Northumbrians (LW ch. 47), who served so long as abbot, and who lived
fully within a monastic context from the day of his first entrance to Lindisfarne until his death

In his portrayal of Wilfrid, Stephen uses the types of apostle and prophet almost interchangeably. That he does so signifies nothing peculiar. While some have seen the type of the Old Testament prophet as more central to his characterization of Wilfrid, and others the New Testament apostle, there is no compelling reason to choose between the two.24 Nor is there any reason to do so. From the point of view of the early Christian imagination, these two types are virtually identical: both Old Testament prophets and New Testament apostles are called by God, both reveal Christ to the world (the apostles openly and the prophets in veiled signs), both work signs and wonders, and both suffer persecution, hardship, and sometimes martyrdom. This last feature, the suffering of persecution and hardship, may stand out as the most significant similarity between these two types and the one which specifically linked them together in the early Christian imagination. Paul, for example, identified his own apostolic experience of persecution with what the prophets experienced (1 Th. 2.14-15). From his perspective, to be either an apostle or a prophet means to suffer.25

Ephesians 2.20 equates these two types when it claims that the church is "built on the foundation of the apostles and prophets." Although the mention of prophets in this passage probably referred originally to early Christian rather than Old Testament prophets, by Stephen's time the distinction between Hebrew and early Christian prophets would have been fully blurred, as perhaps it already was in the New Testament period. To be an Old Testament prophet, a New Testament prophet, or an apostle are

---

some sixty years later, Wilfrid might be expected to be praised more explicitly as a monastic type.

24 For Wilfrid as Old Testament prophet, see the views of Mayr-Harting (141) and Patrick Wormald (in Campbell, *The Anglo-Saxons* 90). For Wilfrid as New Testament apostle, see Isenberg 66-70.

25 Paul's most eloquent testimony to the apostle's life of hardship and persecution can be found in 2 Cor. 11.16-12.10; Paul also makes the identification between prophecy and persecution when he cites the prophet Elijah's appeal to God: "Lord, they have killed thy prophets, they have demolished thy altars, and I alone am left, and they seek my life" (Rom. 11.3). The same identification between the life of a prophet and persecution can be found in every tradition of the New Testament literature, e.g., Mt. 5.12, 23.29-39; Lk. 13.28, 13.34; Acts 7.51-52; Jas. 5.10; Rev. 16.6, 18.24.

typologically equivalent experiences. All involve special dimensions of suffering and persecution.

Whereas the Old Testament narrates in detail the sufferings of the prophets, the New Testament says little about the sufferings of the apostles, except for that of Peter and Paul in the book of Acts. The patristic age, however, soon gave birth to traditions describing the sufferings of all the apostles and the martyrdom of some. The various apocryphal acts of Paul, Peter, Andrew, and Thomas all claim a martyr's end for their respective heroes, while the second-century Gnostic teacher Heracleon knew of only four apostles who did *not* die a martyr's death (H-S 2:43). Throughout late antiquity and the early Middle Ages the tendency to associate apostles with martyrs and confessors remained widespread: to be an apostle also meant to suffer and to be willing to die as a witness for the truth of Christ. Stephen indicates in chapter five, for example, that he knew the apocryphal tradition of Andrew's martyrdom.

Although the era of official persecutions and martyrdom ended with Constantine's elevation to the imperial rank, the ideal of martyrdom remained, but it underwent radical transformation. In place of the old martyr came the new monk, whose austere lifestyle and daily warfare with the demons of his desire was seen as a type of martyrdom. For just as the martyr suffered death at the hands of his or her persecutors, so did the ascetic monk or nun undergo a kind of death through crucifying the flesh and its desires via a life of continual penance. As a consequence, the monk came increasingly to be designated by such terms as *martyr* and *confessor*.26 This tendency to equate the monk with the martyr continued into the early medieval period. The author of the *Anonymous Life of St. Cuthbert*, for example, twice refers to Cuthbert as martyr (4.15, 4.17). He also calls him a confessor, a term which in the early church signified one who had experienced grave bodily danger, but not death, at the hands of persecutors

---

26 Athanasius' *Life of Antony*, for example, speaks of a martyrdom of conscience (ch. 47). On the development of the new spiritual ideal of martyrdom, especially as it relates to Antony, see Malone, *The Monk* 44-46. For a more condensed account of the spiritualizing of martyrdom, see Malone "The Monk."

(LCA 4.16). Obviously the anonymous author intends his readers to construe *martyr* and *confessor* in their later, spiritualized sense.

By curious contrast, when Stephen refers to Wilfrid as confessor, he intends the term in its more primitive, literal sense (chs. 6, 8). Although one might expect a more spiritualized understanding of *confessor* from an early eighth-century monastic author who is writing about a leading monastic figure of the time, that is not what one gets. This consistent depiction of Wilfrid's Christlike suffering in terms of literal persecution by hostile human agents must be reckoned among the most striking features of Stephen's *Life*.27 In this sense, Stephen's *Life* partakes of a spirit wholly foreign to any other early Anglo-Latin saint's Life. Its closest precursors in this sense must be found within an earlier, more militant tradition of Christian apologetic, works such as Tertullian's *Scorpiace*, Lactantius' *The Deaths of the Persecutors*, or Jerome's famous *Letter* 1 to Innocentius about the woman who survived seven blows of the axe.

Such literature sees the demonic element in human life manifesting itself often, though not exclusively or essentially, in secular rulers--Pontius Pilate, the emperors Nero, Decius, or Domitian, for example. This suspicion of secular authority, so common in the early stratum of Christian literature, emerges surprisingly in Stephen's eighth-century work. As often as not, Wilfrid's woes owe their origin to persecuting secular leaders: King Ecgfrith (chs. 24-44), King Aldfrith (chs. 45-58), the Frankish queen Balthild and her dukes (ch. 6), King Oswiu (ch. 14), the Frankish duke Ebroin (ch. 27), Queen Iurminburg (ch. 24), King Aethilred of the Mercians and his queen, and King Centwini of the West Saxons and his queen (ch. 40). Not all temporal rulers whom Wilfrid encounters persecute him. Some, like King Aethilred, banish him only to befriend him later. One must note, however, that whenever Stephen portrays Wilfrid as caught in the throes of a demonic power, he usually suggests a secular ruler as the agent through whom that power becomes effective.

The versions of the apocryphal acts of the apostles, which first appeared in the second and third centuries, provide some of the most

---

27 See appendix IV.

dramatic and vivid accounts of the apostles' struggles with demon-inspired temporal rulers.28 Although Stephen usually draws from the canonical Book of Acts to express the parallels between Wilfrid's experience of persecution and the apostles', he does not shrink from appealing to apocryphal Acts when it serves his purpose. For example, Stephen compares Wilfrid's experience to that of the Apostle John on three separate occasions. In two of them, apocryphal traditions about John provide the inspiration. The first parallel occurs during the episode of Dalfinus' martyrdom. Because Wilfrid offered himself up to be martyred with the Lyon archbishop, Stephen concludes that Wilfrid earned the status of confessor as did John the Apostle and evangelist, "who sat uninjured in a cauldron of boiling oil and drank deadly poison unharmed" (ch. 6). Whereas Tertullian and other Latin writers preserve the tradition of John being boiled in oil,29 there is seemingly only one source for the tradition of drinking the poison unharmed. That source is the *Acts of John* as preserved in an early medieval apocryphal version of the apostolic Acts known as *Pseudo-Abdias*, the only ancient composition which recounts the deeds and deaths of each of the twelve apostles.30 Since the *Pseudo-Abdias* version of John's acts also mentions the boiling-oil tradition, one has good reason for supposing that Stephen had access to the *Pseudo-Abdias* or a work closely related to the tradition which produced it.

The second mention of a parallel between John's and Wilfrid's experience occurs when Wilfrid returns triumphant to Northumbria at the end of the second persecution-deliverance cycle of the justification section

---

28 The apocryphal *Acts of Peter* ch. 41 and *Acts of Paul* 11.3-6 both depict a Satan-inspired Nero as either a hater or murderer of the apostles (H-S 2:321, 384-386); the apocryphal *Acts of Andrew* similarly depict the Roman proconsul Aegeas [=Aegeates] (H-S 2:408-423). In the *Acts of Thomas*, the king Misdaeus has the apostle Thomas slain (H-S 2:526-531).

29 Tertullian, *On Prescription Against Heretics* ch. 36; cf. M. R. James 229.

30 M. R. James thinks that the *Pseudo-Abdias* was compiled in France "not later than the seventh century" (438). Although no English translation of this text exists, a Latin edition can be found in Fabricius 388-742. The account of John being boiled in oil and drinking poison unharmed can be found in *Pseudo-Abdias* 5.2 (Fabricius 533-536) and 5.20 (575-578), respectively. The present author has been able to find little scholarly work on the *Pseudo-Abdias*. The best coverage is in J. P. Migne, ed., *Troisième et Dernière Encyclopédie Théologique*, vol. 24, *Dictionnaire des Apocryphes* (Paris, 1858): 13-20.

(ch. 44). Wilfrid is there likened to "John the Apostle and Evangelist returning from exile to Ephesus...in security and amid the rejoicings of his followers." The same *Pseudo-Abdias* chapter which mentions John's submersion in boiling oil mentions his return to Ephesus, adding also that at Ephesus he had many friends (5.2, 575-576). In identical fashion, Stephen adds that Wilfrid's return occurred amid the rejoicing of his followers.

These almost offhand references to John's trials and his return to Ephesus prove that Stephen and his community knew intimately the apocryphal legends of the apostles. These legends would have made for exciting and relevant mealtime reading in a Benedictine community like Ripon.31 Even those accounts about Peter and Paul which one finds in the canonical Book of Acts can be found in amplified form in the *Pseudo-Abdias*.32 Although one cannot easily ascribe a common theology to the *Abdias* legends, the common theme of persecution permeates nearly all of them. They hold up the old ideal of the martyr and not the newer ideal of the monk, showing that to be a man of God means to be pursued by persecuting authorities.

In paying so much attention to Stephen's comparison of Wilfrid's experience with that of the apostles in the apocryphal Acts, one must not forget that Stephen's characterization of the prophets' and patriarchs' experience is identical to that of the apostles. For Stephen it is no part of faith's task to discern any uniqueness among the several Christ types; on the contrary, faith discerns the common experience that links them together. That experience includes God's call and promise to which the man of God responds in faith, a hopeless situation which makes fulfillment of the promise seem impossible, and God's dramatic intervention to fulfill the promise. Stephen has Wilfrid himself remind his followers of this pattern, assuring them that the seemingly hopeless situations of persecution and exile

---

31 Such reading is recommended in RB 38.1 and 42.3.

32 E.g., Stephen's reference to Paul's revivification of a dead boy can be found both in Acts 20.9-11 and in *Pseudo-Abdias* 2.4 (pp. 446-448), and his reference to Paul's appeal to Caesar in either Acts 25.11 or *Pseudo-Abdias* 2.6 (pp. 449-452).

which they were suffering at King Ecgfrith's hands have been experienced in
the past by all of God's chosen:

> Bear in mind and tell my brethren about the olden days, how
> we read in the Old Law that the patriarchs, beloved of God,
> and Israel His first-born, for four hundred years and more,
> went "from one nation to another, and from one kingdom to
> another," looking for His promise and not despairing. Moses
> and Aaron too and all the prophets of God endured the
> persecution of man, trusting in the Lord. We read also in the
> New Testament that the great Shepherd of the sheep and the
> Head of the whole Church, Jesus Christ, was crucified by the
> Jews and His disciples scattered. Afterwards, throughout the
> whole world, they and their followers after various temptations
> received their crown....(LW ch. 35)

Clinging to the Promise: The Apostolic Teaching of the Roman See

From the perspective of the apostle Paul, justification occurs through
faith. That is, the overcoming of the hopeless situation in which the believer
finds himself or herself comes through clinging to the promises which God
has delivered in revelation: Abraham believed that God would accomplish
his promise of making Abraham the father of many nations even though
Sarah was well past child-bearing years; Christ believed that the God who
justified Abraham would be able to justify him even though he faced
crucifixion, and thus believing, he became "obedient unto death"; finally, Paul
and the early Christians trusted in God's ability to justify them even though
as sinners and transgressors of the law they experienced the hopeless
situation of God's wrath and imminent judgment.

Wilfrid likewise trusts the divine promises implicitly made to him even
when the events of his life seem to be moving in such a way as to nullify those
promises. Seeing the situation through the typological lens bequeathed to
him by Paul and the other New Testament writers, Stephen depicts the
sufferings of Wilfrid and his *familia* as the result of God's judgment, not of
God's betrayal. As Wilfrid himself says to his followers, quoting Hebrews
12.5-6: "My son, despise not thou the chastening of the Lord, nor faint when
thou art rebuked of Him: for whom the Lord loveth He chasteneth, and
scourgeth every son whom He receiveth" (LW ch. 35). From Stephen's point

of view God has handed Wilfrid over to Satan, who is working through the envy of Northumbria's kings and queens to bring him down (LW chs. 21, 24, and 45).

Yet despite God's severe judgment, Wilfrid continues to trust the divine promises originally made to him. Through these promises, God called Wilfrid to become the instrument through whom the divine light would shine upon nearly all the churches of Britain.33 For Wilfrid, to be the bearer of this light required him to fulfill the desire that the Holy Spirit had implanted within him, namely, "to visit the Apostolic See and to learn [there] the rules of ecclesiastical discipline" in order that he might establish those rules throughout all the churches in Britain (ch. 4). Wilfrid fulfilled that desire, weathering sufficient danger in Gaul to earn the title "confessor" and returning to England to begin his divinely appointed commission (chs. 5-7).

Immediately upon his return, Wilfrid fulfills his call to teach ecclesiastical discipline: he instructs King Alhfrith "with keen insight and knowledgeably" about the "varied discipline of the Roman Church order"; at the Synod of Whitby he teaches "with persuasive eloquence" the Roman method for calculating Easter (chs. 7 and 10). Despite Wilfrid's initial successes in fulfilling his call, his faith soon brings him up against implacable foes. As Stephen tells it, the specific object of that faith is the God who, through the teaching and sufferings of the apostles, especially Peter, has set apart the church of Rome as the giver of rules and norms to all the churches of the world. The revelation that God has delivered to Wilfrid, therefore, is the revelation of a New Law, delivered by Christ to Peter and interpreted later through Peter's see. Stephen, moreover, views that later interpretation as possessing an authority hardly less compelling than the original revelation itself. At the core of Wilfrid's faith lies this firm conviction about the later interpretation's all-demanding quality. Through it, God commands unconditional obedience of all who take the call of Christian discipleship seriously.

---

33 LW ch. 1. Stephen continues this image of Wilfrid as a light or fire in chapter five when he describes Wilfrid as a little spark which God fanned to flame. For more on the light imagery used by Stephen in his characterization of Wilfrid, see Isenberg 62-64.

48

Whereas the Northumbrian kings, bishops, abbots, and Archbishop Theodore appear willing to pay lip service to the canons and discipline of the Roman see, Wilfrid settles for nothing less than their complete observance. The good King Aethilred fulfills the Wilfridian ideal in this respect when he says the following about the documents which Wilfrid brings from his last appeal in Rome: "As for the writings of this Apostolic authority I will never in my life disobey a single dot in them..." (ch. 57). Crucial to note here are the words about obedience to Rome's decrees that Stephen puts on Aethilred's lips. Stephen takes them from Jesus' saying about the Law in Matthew 5.18-19:

> For truly, I say to you, till heaven and earth pass away, not an iota, not a dot will pass from the law until all is accomplished. Whoever then relaxes one of the least of these commandments and teaches men so shall be called least in the kingdom of heaven; but he who does them and teaches them shall be called great in the kingdom of heaven.[34]

This parallel with the first evangelist is not simply coincidental. Stephen seems to have special affection for Matthew's gospel. Wilhelm Levison found over twenty places in the *Life* where Stephen either quotes from Matthew directly or refers to an incident which seems to be inspired by a Matthean passage. This number compares with about four referenced passages from Mark and two from Luke.[35]

Stephen's preference for Matthew's gospel may well reflect strong theological and ecclesiological affinities between the two authors. Both authors place issues concerning God's law, its interpretation, and its strict observance at the very heart of their theological message. From the Matthean point of view, Jesus is the new Moses who, in fulfillment of the previous promises found in the Torah, has delivered a verbal revelation

---

34 Vg Mt. 5.18: "Amen quippe dico vobis, donec transeat caelum et terra, iota unum, aut *unus apex* non praeteribit a lege, donec omnia fiant"; cf. LW ch. 57: "Huius apostolicae auctoritatis scriptis ne *unius* quidem litterae *apicem* umquam in vita mea condempnabo..." (italics added).

35 Although Levison did not note that several of the Matthean citations have near or exact parallels in the gospels of Mark and Luke, careful examination of all the Matthean citations will show that many are unique to the first evangelist. Moreover, even when Stephen refers to a passage common to two or all three of the synoptic gospels, his word choice often duplicates Matthew's.

which must be authoritatively interpreted within a carefully organized and structured community of believers. Just as "the scribes and Pharisees" functioned within the Jewish community as the authoritative interpreters of the Old Law of Moses, so will the disciples function as authoritative interpreters of the New Law of Jesus (Perrin 175, 191). First, however, they must be transformed from learning disciples into teaching apostles through their experience of Jesus' resurrection and commissioning of them (Mt. 28). Having undergone that transformation, these first apostles move out into the world in order to teach to all nations all that Jesus has commanded them (Mt. 28.20).

For Stephen and others in the Latin West, Rome became the place particularly associated with the teaching and sufferings of the two most eminent apostles, Paul and especially Peter, who, according to Matthew, received the power of binding and loosing from Christ (Mt 16.18-19). Stephen was well aware of this special charge from Christ to Peter and mentions it five times in the *Life* (chs. 10, 29, 34, 39, and 60). Given Stephen's acknowledgment of the special relation between the original apostles and the Roman see and his endorsement of the Matthean logic concerning the transmission of Christ's authority to successors, it is easy to see how Stephen came to regard the church at Rome as he did.36 For if Christ revealed the New Law to the disciples who became apostles after Christ's resurrection, and if these apostles delivered that Law and authoritatively interpreted it, chiefly in Rome, to a next generation of disciples, then that next generation would also become the transmitter and authoritative interpreter of the Law for still the next generation. And so the process continues *ad infinitum*. From Stephen's point of view, the church of Rome in his time had inherited through the apostles and their successors not only Christ's teachings but also the authority to interpret those teachings. The forms under which both the teachings and their interpretation appeared to later generations included Scripture and such patristic writings and conciliar canons as the church of Rome regarded as orthodox.

---

36 For more on the veneration of the Apostle Peter in seventh- and eighth-century Anglo-Saxon England, see Zwölfer ch. 2.

In his *Life*, Stephen remembers a Wilfrid who took quite seriously the Great Commission's injunction to observe *all* things that Christ commanded both through His own words and through the words of His successors at Rome. Throughout the justification section of the *Life* (chs. 24-55), Wilfrid complains not so much about the violation of his person as about the violation of those *canones, mores, regulae, disciplina, normae,* and *ordines* which the apostolic authority in Rome has firmly established through its councils and traditions (e.g. LW chs. 30, 46, 51). Admittedly, the violations about which he was concerned usually had something to do with his own mistreatment: being despoiled of his monasteries, driven from his see, replaced unlawfully as bishop in Northumbria. Yet Stephen conveys especially well to his readers just what Wilfrid finds so irritating about the kings and bishops who are his enemies. It is not the personal vendetta that they have against him, but rather the audacity by which they embrace certain aspects of Rome's apostolic authority and reject others (LW ch. 46). In failing to do *all* things that Christ commands through the Roman church, they reveal a stubborn disobedience and refuse to acknowledge the all-encompassing claim that God has made upon them in Christ.

Lest anyone confuse the religious issues raised in Stephen's narrative with post-Reformation Protestant/Catholic debates, two points of clarification must be made. First, there can be no question of an idolatrous or uncritical stance toward the pope in this text since Stephen does not depict the pope as the sole vehicle of Rome's apostolic authority. During both accounts of Wilfrid's appeal to the authority of Rome, Stephen gives the impression that a council or synod of bishops decided Wilfrid's case and that the pope served as its mouthpiece. Indeed, no less than 125 bishops are said to have convened to decide Wilfrid's case during his first appeal to Pope Agatho (ch. 53). The basis for the decisions of the Roman church are therefore consensual and it is from their consensual status that they derive their power. That consensus, moreover, is not conceived as being limited to the particular bishops gathered at a particular council. Rather, it includes the will of previous councils, insofar as that will can be discerned through the conciliar decrees. As Pope John himself is made to say before inquiring into Wilfrid's case: "O Holy Synod, first of all it is our duty to go through the canons of our most holy predecessors" (ch. 52). Stephen depicts this consensus as including even the "wise Roman citizens" who, on hearing the opinions of Boniface and Sizentius concerning Wilfrid's case, proclaim themselves in agreement (ch. 53). This public consensual way of settling disputes in Rome contrasts sharply with Stephen's description of the clandestine and conspiratorial way that Wilfrid's fate is decided in England first by King Ecgfrith and Archbishop Theodore, and later by King Aldfrith and the greedy bishops at Austerfield (chs. 24, 47).

Secondly, from Stephen's viewpoint the conflict between Wilfrid and his opponents involves more than competing partisan viewpoints--one Roman, one non-Roman. The problem with Kings Ecgfrith, Aldfrith, and Wilfrid's episcopal opponents is not simply their refusal to submit to the judgments of this or that earthly council, but their unwillingness to obey radically a transcendent authority. One might wish to argue from the point of view of external history that Wilfrid's opponents indeed acknowledged a transcendent authority, and that the real argument was over where it is most fully and authoritatively revealed. Wilfrid saw it as being revealed through the universal Church as represented by the Petrine tradition of Rome; his opponents through the Celtic Church as represented by the Johannine tradition of Iona (EH 3.25). However historically true that picture may be, it does not fit Stephen's literary and theological purposes to depict the struggle in that way. For him, refusal to bow to a Roman synod's canonical decree signifies a far more dire refusal to humble oneself before God. Worldly desire rather than divine reverence motivates Wilfrid's enemies: Ecgfrith is moved by envy, Archbishop Theodore and his other episcopal opponents by greed.37

Obedient Son and Commanding Father

In the final chapter of this book we shall explore the deeper existential significance of Stephen's characterization of Wilfrid as an imitator

---

37 Ecgfrith is depicted as having been infected by the envy [*invidia*] of his queen (LW ch. 24); Theodore as having been bribed (LW ch. 24); and the other bishops as motivated by avarice [*avaritia*] (LW ch. 46).

of Christ in the mold of the apostles and the prophets and of Stephen's primitive theology of persecution. By discussing Wilfrid as the one who imitates Christ in his roles as persecuted apostle and prophet, this chapter has highlighted the emphasis that Stephen placed upon him as one who suffers and who faithfully submits himself to suffering. From a Trinitarian perspective, it is possible to see Wilfrid as one who imitates God the Son, who in turn humbled Himself in obedience to the will of God the Father. Yet as every student of Stephen's *Life* knows, Wilfrid is depicted as more than simply the obedient son who radically submits himself to the will of God. Indeed, the dominant image of Wilfrid which most readers of the *Life* carry away with them is that of Wilfrid the powerful father who builds magnificent churches, wields great authority, protects his monastic *familia*, instructs the sons of nobles, and counsels kings. How can the two images be reconciled? How can Stephen depict Wilfrid both as obedient son and as commanding father? By depicting Wilfrid as a powerful father who wields worldly as well as spiritual authority, does he not risk nullifying all his attempts to present Wilfrid as a model of the obedient, suffering servant? Such questions require a more detailed examination of Stephen's depiction of Wilfrid as father, of the father-son dynamic which permeates Stephen's narrative, and of whether or not the depiction of Wilfrid as father can be understood as anything other than an aberration of the Christ-type.

CHAPTER THREE

WILFRID AS TYPE OF CHRIST (II)--
PIUS PATER

The Father-Son Dialectic in Stephen's *Life*

During Wilfrid's last exile under King Aldfrith in the 690s, Aldhelm, the great abbot of Malmesbury and bishop of Sherbourne, wrote a letter to Wilfrid's abbots encouraging them to suffer along with Wilfrid in lonely exile. Appealing to their deepest filial impulses he writes:

> For what toil, I ask, is so hard and cruel as to divide and shut you off from the bishop who, nourishing, teaching, reproving, raised you in fatherly love from the very beginning of your first studies and from the early infancy of tender years to the flower of adult manhood; and like a nurse bearing and reviving her loved fosterlings in her warm embrace, mercifully clasped and cherished you in the bosom of his love? (Whitelock, *C. 597-1042* 793-794; orig. in MGH AA 15:500-502)

Aldhelm's moving appeal reveals how the father-son relationship functioned as a powerful metaphor for describing the ties that bound monk to abbot and priest to bishop in Late Antique and early medieval piety. In the *Life of Bishop Wilfrid*, Stephen, like Aldhelm, takes pains to cast Wilfrid in the role of a loving father who exercises a paternal authority and care over his priests and abbots, and over certain kings. Before examining the particular way in which Stephen portrays Wilfrid's fatherly bearing, we must first consider more generally how he understands the father-son dialectic, how that dialectic governs the relations between different characters in his *Life*, and the place that it occupies in Stephen's larger theology.

The existence of parity relationships within the *Life*, that is, relationships between equals and friends, is rarely found. Its social world is one of strict hierarchy in which each character occupies his or her proper place in relation to the others. But that hierarchy is not static. As the central character, Wilfrid moves from a position of subordination at the narrative's beginning to one of authority at its end. His movement toward authority is depicted as the direct result of the way that he humbled himself to a higher divine authority which God wields through various human vicegerents. As the last chapter showed, Stephen portrays Wilfrid as one who--in imitation of Christ, the apostles and prophets--submitted to God's sovereign will and thereby suffered persecution. This human submission to the divine will, however, imitates divinity itself by replicating the eternal identification of the Son's will with the Father's (cf. Mt. 7.21; Jn. 6.38). Whatever else Christlikeness might be for Stephen, it is obedience first (cf. Isenberg 81-88).

Stephen wastes no time in establishing Wilfrid's exceptional obedience and humility. Chapter two opens by praising Wilfrid's obedience to his parents (*parentibus obediens*). Being "swift to hear, slow to speak" (Jas. 1.19), he humbly ministers "to all who came to his father's house," be they the king's companions or their slaves. To serve all in this way recalls to Stephen's mind a passage from the prophet Isaiah by way of John's Gospel: "All shall be taught by the Lord" (Jn. 6.45; cf. Is. 54.13). Although it is not clear what Stephen means to signify with this scriptural citation, the word "all" in his narrative, referring to "all" (*omnibus*) who came to Wilfrid's father's house, seems meant to be taken as parallel to the "all" (*omnes*) of the scriptural citation (i.e., "All shall be taught by the Lord"). This would seem to imply that for Stephen all who come to Wilfrid's father's house, both those of high estate and of low, are being taught by the Lord through Wilfrid's ministrations to them. Wilfrid's example of humility and obedience becomes an epiphany of who God is for them and what God demands of them.

Obediently obtaining his father's blessing, Wilfrid obtains permission to make his way to Northumbria's Queen Eanflaed so that he might "serve

God under her counsel and protection."1 Eanflaed, in turn, bids Wilfrid to minister to Cudda, a paralytic nobleman who has embraced the monastic life at Lindisfarne. Because Wilfrid accepts and performs this task with such diligence, both Cudda and the senior monks at Lindisfarne come to regard the youth "like a son."2 In addition, while serving Cudda, Wilfrid submitted himself "with deep reverence of heart, in humility and obedience" to the monastic discipline at Lindisfarne. In ministering to Cudda and serving God through conformity to the monastic life, Wilfrid fulfills, in Stephen's mind, the example of the young Samuel when he ministered to Eli the priest (1 Sam. 3.1).

These metaphors of sonship and obedience emerge with even greater intensity in the story of Wilfrid's relationship with Archbishop Dalfinus of Lyon (LW chs. 4 and 6). As the previous chapter showed, Stephen depicted Wilfrid as a latter-day type of the persecuted prophet and apostle. By describing Wilfrid's relations with the martyr Dalfinus in terms of a father-son dialectic, he expresses his conviction that the two were kindred spirits and Wilfrid, from the very beginning of his holy career, had the mind of a martyr. "Nothing could be better for us," says young Wilfrid to Dalfinus, "than that father and son die together and be with Christ" (LW ch. 6). Of course, Wilfrid does not die, but by wishing to suffer along with his father Wilfrid is established as one who by intention, if not by deed, has earned the glory of the martyr's crown. The fate of the father thus partly foreshadows the fate of the son: Wilfrid, too, will become a bishop who is persecuted by a secular ruler.

Stephen continues to underscore Wilfrid's precocious obedience and humility until chapter fourteen, when Wilfrid at last occupies the Northumbrian see at York. Up until that point, Wilfrid has fully submitted himself to the instruction, counsel, and care of several mentors: his own father, Queen Eanflaed, Cudda, the older monks at Lindisfarne, King

---

1 Foreshadowing the later theme of persecution, chapter two mentions that Wilfrid suffers from a cruel stepmother.

2 LW ch. 2: "quasi filius."

Erconberht of Kent, Archbishop Dalfinus, St. Andrew, the Roman archdeacon Boniface, and the pope.

In chapter fourteen, however, Stephen begins to transform Wilfrid-the-son into Wilfrid-the-father. Indeed, Wilfrid will function primarily as father to others, especially to the English church, throughout the rest of the *Life*. What has always struck readers as so remarkable about Stephen's portrait of Wilfrid is the broad scope of Wilfrid's fatherly authority. That authority appears in his varying roles: as teacher, provider, and man of respect among priests, abbesses, his abbots and monks; as counselor and guardian to kings and queens; and as teacher, evangelizer, and benefactor of the laity.3 Although he can properly be called a spiritual father, that term must be understood in its broadest conceivable sense. For Stephen does not present him to us simply, or even primarily, as the wise abbot who instructs his monks in the secrets of the spiritual life. More often, Wilfrid busies himself with the more rudimentary and public tasks of building churches, almsgiving, preaching, protecting, ordaining, and setting the churches of Britain firmly within the liturgical and canonical tradition of the universal church as that tradition had been authoritatively defined through the apostolic see of Rome.

The Theological Significance of Wilfrid's Fatherly Role

Performing such functions, Stephen's Wilfrid often looms large as a man of power and largess--a figure not to be toyed with. Such an image may not always seem to fit well with Stephen's image of Wilfrid as suffering servant, apostle, and prophet, for the latter image implies being scorned, rejected, and humiliated, whereas the former implies just the opposite. What should the sensitive reader make of this juxtaposition of images? By

---

3 On Wilfrid's fatherly relations to priests, abbesses, and his abbots, see LW chs. 21, 47, 62(63) and 63(64); to kings and nobility, LW chs. 7 (Alhfrith of Deira), 21, 28 and 33 (Dagobert), 41 (King Aethilwalh of Sussex), 42 (Caedwalla of Wessex), 47 (one of King Aldfrith's thegns), 59 (Osred of Northumbria), and 63(64) (Ceolred of Mercia); to laity and the church in general, Wilfrid functions as evangelizer (LW ch. 26), provider/protector (8, 11, 21), teacher (11, 26) and builder/repairer of churches (16, 17, 22).

depicting Bishop Wilfrid as fatherly lord who possesses riches and is attended by a "countless army of followers arrayed in royal vestments and arms" (LW ch. 24), does Stephen show his true colors as one who finally could not exchange the old Germanic ideal of the warrior-hero for the new Christian hero whose weakness is his strength and whose wealth is his poverty?4 How can Stephen expect the reader to accept Wilfrid both as the father who rebukes, teaches, and protects and as the son who obediently submits himself to humiliation? Such objections require serious attention. Indeed, they are raised not only by the thoughtful reader of Stephen's *Life*, but by the New Testament itself, which typically associates Christ with the obedience of sonship, and never with fatherhood. For the image of the father, when applied to humans, always carries with it the danger of idolatry: "And call no man your father on earth, for you have one Father, who is in heaven" (Mt. 23.9).

Yet, as in so much else, Stephen takes his cue from the apostle Paul. In 1 Corinthians 4, Paul applies the fatherly epithet to himself in describing his relations with the church at Corinth, which was established through his preaching. Reproving certain Corinthians for their arrogance in claiming to have a greater status in Christ than their brethren, he writes:

> Already you are filled! Already you have become rich! Without us you have become kings! And would that you did reign, so that we might share the rule with you! For I think that God has exhibited us apostles as last of all, like men sentenced to death; because we have become a spectacle to the world, to angels and to men....I do not write this to make you ashamed, but to admonish you as my beloved children. For though you have countless guides in Christ, you do not have many fathers. For I became your father in Christ Jesus through the gospel. I urge you, then, be imitators of me. (1 Cor. 4.8-9, 4.14-16)

Calling the Corinthians' pretensions into question, Paul asserts that his own apostolic status derives not from his superior worldly wisdom, wealth, or power, but from his suffering--from being last of all, sentenced to death, a spectacle to the world. Moreover, his apostolic status, which derives from his

---

4 On the comparision of Wilfrid's qualities with those of a secular lord and hero, see Campbell 173-175, Wormald 54-55, and Mayr-Harting 228. For earlier memorable depictions of Wilfrid in this way, see R. H. Hodgkin 346 and Thomas Hodgkin 213.

Christlike suffering, legitimates his claim to be the Corinthians' father in Christ and not just their guide. Because he has been called as an apostle and because that call has received the seal of authenticity through his Christlike suffering, Paul exercises a fatherly authority appropriate to his apostolic status. One might say paradoxically that because Paul conforms to the image of obedient son, he becomes spiritual father to the Corinthians and, as such, properly exercises a fatherly authority over them. But what does Paul mean when he says, "I became your father in Christ Jesus through the gospel. I urge you, then, be imitators of me"? Does he mean that they should imitate his fatherly authority? He cannot mean that, at least not in any conventional sense, for he has already indicated that the Corinthians' greatest problem is their wish to lord it over others in the way that fathers lord it over their children. By exhorting them to be his imitators, Paul rather beckons them to participate in his own apostolic--and Christlike--experience of suffering and persecution. Such suffering is the definitive criterion for the Christian life and the only way that the privilege of fatherly authority is divinely conferred. In other words, the glorification which the fatherly privilege bespeaks is not something to be seized (Phil. 2.6-7). It comes rather as a gift which God confers on those who, though despised as sinners and scoundrels by the world, submit themselves to the divine will and to the humiliation that inevitably comes with it.

Just as Paul regards his fatherly authority as deriving from his apostolic suffering, so does Stephen view Wilfrid's fatherly authority as deriving from his suffering and humiliation. By patiently enduring his stepmother's cruelty; by faithfully obeying his father, Queen Eanflaed, Cudda, King Erconberht, and Archbishop Dalfinus; by ministering to kings and slaves alike; by weathering the ordeal of pilgrimage; and--most of all--by freely submitting himself to the dangers of martyrdom in Gaul, Wilfrid shows himself to be an imitator of apostolic suffering.

Moreover, because he imitates the apostle's suffering so consistently, Wilfrid comes to receive the apostle's fatherly privilege which God alone confers. By placing the stories about Wilfrid's friendship with King Alhfrith, his installation as abbot at Ripon, and his ordination as priest immediately after the story of his difficult childhood and pilgrimage, Stephen indicates that the later blessings are linked to the earlier ordeals. As if the strong implication were not enough, he explicitly describes Wilfrid's life before abbatial and priestly ordination as his days of poverty (*paupertas*) and trials (*angustiae*) and his life afterwards as comparable to the experience of the young Samuel who, "after many tribulations, was judged worthy to receive the gift of prophecy."[5] Like Samuel, Wilfrid has undergone many tribulations in obedience to his divine calling, thus proving his status as man of God. Having thus pointed beyond himself, Wilfrid is glorified by that toward which he points. Paraphrasing God's words from the same Samuel story, Stephen articulates the essential principle at work in Wilfrid's elevation to fatherly status: "He who honors me, I shall honor."[6]

Just as Paul's exhortation of the Corinthians to imitate him excludes a direct imitation of his fatherly power, so would imitation of Wilfrid exclude direct imitation of his grand leadership style. As we mentioned in an earlier chapter, the imitation of a saint has two dimensions. The first has to do with conscious imitation of behavior, the second with the mere recognition and conviction that what one has experienced through the power of God is comparable to what has happened to earlier types--the prophets, Christ, the apostles, the saints--in whom that same divine power was at work. In 1 Corinthians 4 and in Stephen's *Life*, one is exhorted to imitate the holy man's humiliation in the first, behavioral sense. For both authors imitation in the second, convictional sense does not result from any direct human initiative. It happens *to* the believer. Just as the human Christ obediently took up his cross, but did not resurrect himself--he was resurrected by the power of God --so do Paul and Wilfrid obediently submit to apostolic suffering, but do not directly make themselves fathers. The latter happens to them through God's power alone. Stephen intends by implication for the reader who wishes to imitate St. Wilfrid to imitate his suffering and not his fatherly glory. For just

---

5 LW ch. 8: "ostendens perspicue, quid animo gerebat in paupertate...."; LW ch. 9: "Deo concedente et in angustiis suis custodiente...."

6 LW ch. 16 (author's translation); cf. 1 Sam. 2.30. In place of the Latin verb for "to glorify" (=*glorifico*), which the Vulgate uses in 1 Sam. 2.30, Stephen uses here the verb for "to honor" (=*honorifico*).

as Wilfrid refused to exercise the immense human authority that his "father" Dalfinus offered him, but remained content to love the archbishop from the humble status of sonship, so should the imitators of Wilfrid do the same (LW chs. 4 and 6). Perhaps, like Wilfrid, Wilfrid's imitators will be elevated to a father-like authority. That elevation, however, can be none of their concern. It belongs solely to the province of God.

If the one who suffers obediently as son can also receive fatherly authority, then, by implication, Christ himself also enjoys a fatherly authority. Although the New Testament never ascribes the title of *father* to Christ, the Church Fathers obviously did not regard this New Testament omission as proscriptive. A vigorous tradition concerning the fatherhood of Christ began in the second century with Justin Martyr and continued in the writings of Origen, Ambrose, Augustine, and others.7

When considered as part of the Triune Godhead itself, Christ was associated with the Son and the Son alone. Yet when considered as the foundation of the church which declared him Lord, he could be properly regarded as father. The human Christ's fatherhood, however, differs from that of God the Father in that the authority of the former derives from the latter: it is God who raises up Jesus from the dead. By contrast, the Father's authority is self-derived. In Christlike fashion, the fatherhood of Paul and the other Christian apostles, prophets, and teachers, is not self-derived, but is derived from the Christ, who is glorified at the Father's right hand. Drawing upon Paul's identification of the apostolic with the fatherly role, early Christians began to interpret the pastoral and administrative roles, especially that of bishop, with the help of fatherly language. In the second-century *Martyrdom of Polycarp*, Bishop Polycarp of Smyrna is denounced as the "father of the Christians" (12.2). From there the fatherly designation for the bishop gains widespread currency both in the Greek East and Latin West. By the seventh century the special status of the Roman bishop will issue in

---

7 Justin Martyr, *Dialogue against Trypho* ch. 123; Origen, *Homilies on Exodus* 6.2; Augustine *Tractates on the Gospel of John* ch. 75 (on John 14.18-21). For more references and a fuller discussion of the patristic tradition of the fatherhood of Christ, see RB/1980 356-361.

the ascription to him of a special fatherly title: *papa*.8 Besides bishops, leaders of monastic communities acquire the fatherly designation of *abbot*, which derives from *abba*, an Aramaic word for father (e.g., Mk. 14.36, Gal. 4.6, Rom. 8.15).

The Spiritual Father as Teacher

Since Wilfrid had been both bishop and abbot, Stephen had double reason to apply the fatherly epithets liberally to him. But what, for Stephen, did it mean to be a good or loving father in the spiritual sense? And what duties did it entail? First and foremost, it meant to be a good teacher. Stephen presents Wilfrid's first pilgrimage to Rome largely as a teacher-training mission. When Archbishop Dalfinus offers Wilfrid a large part of Gaul to rule, Wilfrid refuses by proclaiming that he has vowed to "learn the rules of ecclesiastical discipline" in Rome so that the English would "grow in the service of God" (LW ch. 4). That is, Wilfrid sees his call as including a specific charge to teach Roman discipline to the English. Once in Rome, he proceeds to the oratory of St. Andrew and there prays that God will grant him "a mind for the reading and an eloquence for the teaching of the Gospels among the nations," and this prayer is said to be fulfilled. For from Rome's archdeacon Boniface he learns the four Gospels perfectly, the rule for dating Easter, and "many other rules of ecclesiastical discipline" (LW ch. 5). In addition, on his way home in Lyon, he "learned many things from the most learned teachers" (LW ch. 6).

Once home in Northumbria, Wilfrid is elevated to the offices of abbot, then priest, then bishop. Stephen makes it clear that Wilfrid's accession to these ranks owed much to his superior knowledge and authority as teacher. In chapter seven the young King Alhfrith is said to have summoned Wilfrid to him because he knew that Wilfrid had learned the "manifold discipline of the church of Saint Peter the Apostle." On greeting Alhfrith, Wilfrid proceeds immediately to teach him the scriptural basis for the greeting of peace. His knowledge on such matters so impresses Alhfrith

---

8 On the early designation of bishop as father, see Neuhäuser; on the evolution of the title *pope* for the bishop of Rome, see Labriolle.

that the king invites him to stay so that he may preach to both Alhfrith and all the people. He also grants Wilfrid the monastery at Ripon, whereupon Wilfrid is ordained abbot (LW ch. 8). A little later, Stephen depicts Wilfrid, now a priest, as the heroic spokesman for the Roman party at the Synod of Whitby (LW ch. 10). With a "sweet-spoken eloquence," Wilfrid instructs the assembled crowd on the Roman system for dating Easter and convinces King Oswiu to accept that system as authoritative. Immediately after his account of the Synod of Whitby, Stephen relates that Wilfrid was elected to the bishopric. Among the several criteria for a bishop which the kings and their counsellors are said to have considered, Stephen mentions first and foremost a willingness "to observe...the discipline of the Apostolic See and to teach it to others." The kings decide that Wilfrid best fulfills that criterion, being "wise in all matters," and so they elect him to the bishopric "to teach God's law" (LW ch. 11).

Throughout the rest of the *Life*, Stephen depicts Wilfrid again and again as teacher and preacher *par excellence*. At one moment Wilfrid is teaching the sons of nobles, at the next exhorting the heathen through his powerful preaching (LW chs. 21, 26). At the Council of Austerfield, Wilfrid is portrayed reminding his opponents of his greatest achievements, all of which concern his teaching of Roman ways and customs to an England which, prior to Wilfrid's teaching activity, knew nothing of them.9 Even at his death, Wilfrid is shown to have had teaching at the forefront of his mission. According to Stephen, the old bishop dies en route to Mercia's King Ceolred who, in Wilfrid's words, "has promised to order his entire life after my instruction."10

While it is true to claim that, for Stephen, Wilfrid's teaching authority derived from his fatherly status, that may tell only half the story. Stephen probably believed that authority also derived from Wilfrid's perfect imitation of the prophet and apostle type. Such an interpretation of both a bishop's and

---

9 LW ch. 47; in particular, Wilfrid here mentions his teaching of the Easter dating, the correct form of the Roman tonsure, the use of a double choir singing in harmony, and the Benedictine rule.

10 LW ch. 63(64): "qui enim omnem vitam suam meo iudicio disponere promittit."

an abbot's teaching authority was well known to the western monastic tradition that Stephen represents. Its most eloquent expression comes from the *Rule of the Master* which Benedict himself probably used extensively in composing his own rule. In the very first chapter of his work, the Master discusses the resources for teaching which the Church has had and continues to have at her disposal for carrying out Christ's will on earth. He writes,

> Now, the Lord has given his Church, in conformity with the Trinity, three series of teaching: first, that of the prophets; secondly, that of the apostles; thirdly, that of the Fathers. According to their authority and teaching, the churches and schools of Christ are governed. (RM 1.82-83)

According to the Master, the Church has been taught in successive ages by the Old Testament prophets, the New Testament apostles, and the Fathers. The prophets taught before Christ, the apostles immediately after, and the Fathers in the present age. But who are the Fathers? They are the governors of the "churches" and the "schools of Christ," namely the bishops and their subordinates, who rule the churches on the one hand, and the abbots and their subordinates who rule the schools of Christ, or monasteries, on the other.11 The Master thus expresses the conviction that in the present age both bishops and abbots continue the work which the prophets and apostles did in former ages. He goes on to emphasize the centrality of the teaching role for the life of the Church:

> Therefore all who still have folly as their mother ought to be subject to the authority of a superior so that, guided on their way by the judgment of a teacher, they may avoid the way of self-will. The Lord gives us his commands through a teacher since, as he said above, he is always with these teachers, to the end of time, certainly for no other purpose than to instruct us through them. As the Lord himself says to his disciples who are our teachers: 'Anyone who listens to you listens to me; anyone who rejects you rejects me.' Thus if we put into practice what we hear from these teachers, we no longer do our own will, so that on the day of judgment the devil will have in us no basis to claim us for himself in hell, because the Lord has always accomplished in us what will be judged worthy of glory. (RM 1.87-92)

---

11 The role of bishops and abbots as the heads of their respective households is stated more explicitly in RM 11.5-14.

Citing Luke 10.16, the Master reminds his audience that those who reject the teachers, which include the Lord's disciples and, by implication, present-day bishops and abbots, reject the Lord himself. For him the great evil of the Christian life is self-will and its remedy is the willful submission to Christ's representatives on earth, namely, bishops and abbots.

Although it could never be convincingly argued that Stephen knew the *Rule of the Master*, it can be said that his understanding of Wilfrid as apostle, prophet, teacher, father, bishop, and abbot conform so closely to it that he must have caught its spirit somewhere. Perhaps such ideas about ecclesiastical authority simply belonged to a common fund of western monastic tradition. While the *Rule of St. Benedict* fails to forge such a theologically elegant link between the teachings of the prophets and apostles of old and the teachings of present-day abbots and bishops, its teaching about abbatial authority echoes the Master's strong theology of subordination. According to Benedict's *Rule*, the abbot exercises the authority of Christ over his monks and, in parallel fashion, Christ exercises authority as *paterfamilias* over the abbot and holds him accountable both for his teaching and for his monks' obedience (RB 2.1-10). Since the abbot holds the place of Christ, his monks must obey his every word. Not to do so is to reject Christ himself.

In accordance with the spirit of the *Rules* of the Master and St. Benedict, Stephen knew that Wilfrid, as both bishop and abbot, exercised the teaching authority in an extraordinary way. What strikes the reader as curious, however, is just how little Stephen mentions Wilfrid's specifically abbatial authority and teaching. In those frequent mentions of Wilfrid's teaching activity, Stephen usually portrays kings and the laity, not monks, as his pupils. What Wilfrid seems most concerned to teach--namely, the Gospels and the rules of church discipline (LW ch. 5)--belong more appropriately to the secular church than to the monastery. To be sure, Stephen does mention briefly that Wilfrid taught his monasteries to observe the Benedictine *Rule*, to adopt the Petrine form of the tonsure, and to use a double choir, but for the most part, he emphasizes Wilfrid's work in the secular church (LW ch. 47). Even when Wilfrid emerges as the spiritual father of his monks, he does so more as one who administers to them the milk of doctrine rather than its solid food. Never as abbot does he function as private confessor or spiritual guide. Never does he utter a pithy saying or perform a parabolic action in the manner of the Desert Fathers. He always teaches publicly, formally--imparting fundamentals, enforcing regulations. Stephen perhaps summarizes Wilfrid's teaching mission to the Church best when he says: "He adorned her [i.e., the Church] fairly with the rules of discipline as with the flowers of virtue, making her chaste and modest, continent, temperate and submissive, clothing her in many hues" (LW ch. 17). Such are *Bishop* Wilfrid's special concerns in his teaching function as father.

The Spiritual Father as Provider and Protector

Although Wilfrid's fatherly authority requires him, above all else, to teach, it includes other duties. Perhaps providing for and protecting the poor and the powerless rank as most important after teaching. As provider for both clergy and laity Wilfrid is said to have no equal (LW ch. 21). He gives alms liberally to the poor, orphans, and widows (chs. 8, 11); he provides sumptuous churches for worship. Even on his deathbed, Wilfrid concerns himself with the welfare of his various children, allotting one quarter of his treasury for the poor, one quarter for his monastic *familiae* at Ripon and Hexham, and one quarter for landless men who suffered in exile with him (LW ch. 62(63)). Continuing the ways of his "father" Wilfrid, Ripon's Abbot Tatberht observes the anniversary of Wilfrid's death by distributing the tithes from the herds and flocks to the poor among the people (LW ch. 64(65)).

Perhaps more than other hagiographers, Stephen possesses an acute sensitivity to the hostile forces which besiege human life at every turn. Such sensitivity leads to an extraordinary concern in his *Life* for the protection of innocents from hostile, Satanic powers. As a youth vulnerable to danger and persecution, Wilfrid himself is said to have enjoyed the protection of God through such human and non-human agents as Archbishop Dalfinus, holy relics, King Perctarit of Campania, St. Peter, King Aethilwalh, King Aethilred, and the holy apostles.[12] As one whom God has raised to the

---

12 Archbishop Dalfinus (ch. 4); holy relics (chs. 5, 7); King Perctarit of Campania (ch. 28); St Peter (chs. 33, 50, 53); King Aethilwalh (ch. 41); King Aethilred (ch. 45); and the holy apostles (ch. 50).

fatherly rank of bishop and abbot, Wilfrid himself functions as a divine agent of protection. He teaches King Ecgfrith to "guard his land and defend the churches of God" (LW ch. 20); he protects the exiled King Dagobert (LW ch. 33); he nurtures children in the cradle (LW ch. 47); he adopts young King Osred as his son (LW ch. 59). Indeed, one might argue that Wilfrid's zeal for teaching ecclesiastical rules and discipline grows out of his more fundamental desire to protect the incipient English church from the wanton rapacity of secular and spiritual rulers.

In Stephen's *Life*, Wilfrid's powers of protection reach their height after his death. Of the saint's three posthumous miracles, two are miracles of protection. In the first, an angel of the Lord defends the building at Oundle, where Wilfrid died, from arsonists (LW ch. 66(67)). In the second, a white arc in the twilight sky encircles the Ripon monastery. For Stephen that arc signifies a "wall of divine help" around the monastic *familia* which Wilfrid had fathered on both sides of the Humber. This supernatural wall not only wards off the arrows of enemies, but sends them hurtling back to their source! Its presence signifies that Wilfrid has been glorified by God to a status "equal to the Apostles of God, Peter and Andrew, whom he specially loved" (LW ch. 67(68)). For just as Wilfrid, so vulnerable in life to the assaults of his enemies, enjoyed the apostolic protection of Sts. Peter and Andrew, so now does his *familia*, still vulnerable to those same dangers, enjoy the equal protection of Wilfrid glorified. Thus, the cycle of salvation moves on to a new generation. Just as Peter and Andrew and the other apostles preached, became "fathers" to those who believed, suffered persecution, died and were glorified, so do such of their "children" as Wilfrid obediently take up the call to preach and teach, become "fathers" themselves, suffer persecution, die, and become glorified. These latter in turn become examples for their children in the same way that Peter and Andrew were for Wilfrid.

Surely Stephen understood that Wilfrid's special devotion to Sts. Peter and Andrew had its origin not merely in their direct personal intervention in his life, but more especially in the aid they offered him through the power of the apostolic see of Rome.13 Wilfrid visits Rome three times in Stephen's *Life*, and during his last two visits is vindicated by the apostolic authority of the pope and his synod. In chapter thirty Wilfrid speaks of Rome's apostolic see as a fortified place (*locum munitum*) and a tower of strength (*turremque fortitudinis*) where, by virtue of the sacred canons which it upholds (*normam sacrorum canonum*), he could receive a righteous judgment. One notes how Wilfrid's use of fortress-image to describe the apostolic see mirrors Stephen's concluding image of a "wall of divine help" which shields Wilfrid's *familia* from its enemies. Like the protection which Wilfrid receives through the apostolic Roman church, the fatherly protection that he gives to the English churches is largely the protection of law. By adorning them with the rules of discipline, as Stephen says in chapter seventeen, that is, by teaching them God's law as it had been revealed to all the churches of the world through the apostolic see of Rome, Wilfrid provides protection for the English churches in the same way that the apostolic martyrs and their successors provided the same for Rome's once-persecuted church. Like all good fathers, Wilfrid lays down the law for his children--not a law of his own making, but the law of *his* fathers, a law that ultimately derives from the New Law which God the Father revealed in Christ and which Christ transmitted to the church through the apostles and the saints.

The Spiritual Father as a Man of Power

As father, Wilfrid not only teaches, provides, and protects, he also displays a sometimes fearsome and commanding might. One of Stephen's most haunting images is found in chapter eighteen. There Stephen relates how Bishop Wilfrid goes out one day among the people to baptize and confirm. While making his rounds, he meets a woman sorely grieved by the death of her first-born infant son. Having hidden the corpse of her child in swaddling clothes, she exposes its face in the hope that Wilfrid, by confirming

---

13 Peter's associations with Rome are clear enough, but Andrew also enjoyed a popular cult in Rome during the early Middle Ages. See Levison 72 and LW$_2$ 198, n. 1.

it, might bring it back to life. Hesitating at first, Wilfrid at last yields to the mother's pitiful pleadings. As Wilfrid prays and places his hand upon the dead child's body, the child revives and is immediately baptized by the bishop. Returning the babe to the grateful mother, Wilfrid commands her in God's name to return the boy to him at age seven for the service of God. When the mother later sees how handsome her boy grows to be, she reneges on her promise, and flees with her son from the country. Wilfrid commisions his *praefectus*, Hocca, to go out and search for the boy. Having found the child hidden among others of the British race, Hocca brings him back "by force" (*coacte*) to Wilfrid. The boy is received into the bishop's *familia*, given the surname *Filius Episcopi* (= Bishop's Son) and is said to have remained at Ripon serving God for the rest of his life.

Perhaps this simple narrative dramatizes better than any other the *Life of Wilfrid*'s sometimes disturbing vision of what spiritual sonship and fatherhood entail. In this episode as in others throughout the *Life*, to be a son means to have life through and only through the life-giving agency of a father. In its generative function, human fatherhood recalls and signifies the more fundamental Fatherhood of God the Creator. As faithful imitator of God, Wilfrid too confers a fullness of life--natural and spiritual--upon his various "children," be they this dead boy, his monastic and clerical *familia*, kings like Osred and Caedwalla, or the entire English people.

Yet for Stephen, spiritual fatherhood implies more than a simple privilege of generativity. It brings with it grave responsibilities for teaching and enforcing discipline. Stephen focuses so intensely upon this latter, more difficult aspect of fatherhood that it might be said to provide the central conflict around which his entire narrative revolves. For in chapter after chapter, Wilfrid will appear as a spiritual mentor who tries to discipline divers sons and daughters, some of whom seem all but intractable. By thus refusing to sentimentalize father-son relations, Stephen's narrative sets forth for its audience the demanding requirements of sonship, foremost of which is humble obedience.

If the bishop-child relation in chapter eighteen functions as a type for divine-human relations, it then follows that divine election, typified here by restoration of the boy's life, always implies a subsequent discipline. The care that God shows to humanity through his servant Wilfrid always includes the enforcing of discipline as well as the conferring of blessing. Attempts to avoid that discipline are shown to be at best futile, as they prove to be in this story, and at worst fatal, as they are for King Aldfrith (LW ch. 59). For such discipline is energized by nothing less than God's unconditional--and therefore awesome--command to obey. In its unconditionality that command is addressed equally to each individual. As one commissioned by God to be bishop, Wilfrid does not rest content to enforce discipline among this or that class, order, rank or race. He demands that kings as well as clergy observe the sacred canons and that they order their lives after his instruction; he evangelizes Mercians as well as Northumbrians, South Saxons as well as West Saxons, Frisians as well as Anglo-Saxons; he brooks no opposition to divine law, be that opposition from Archbishop Theodore or from a lowly mother who has made a promise she comes to regret. In short, Wilfrid casts wide the net of his fatherly authority.

But to what end? It has been said of Augustine's archfoe Pelagius that he wanted every Christian to be a monk (Brown, *Augustine* 348). The same might be said of Stephen's Wilfrid, though with some qualification. Whereas for Pelagius every Christian's imitation of the monk meant nothing less than to strive ceaselessly for absolute moral perfection, for Stephen's Wilfrid it meant to live faithfully under a rule. Just as every good monk consented to live under the rule of his monastery in accordance with his abbot's commands, so too, Stephen's *Life* would tell us, should every baptized man and woman consent to live under the rule of the Church in accordance with the canons, laws and discipline that have emanated from God through Christ, from Christ through the apostles, and from the apostles to the universal church whose authoritative mouthpiece is the church in Rome.

If Stephen's *Life* does indeed see every man and woman as obliged by God to live under some rule, then its reticence about things specifically monastic seems less strange. For according to the convictions of the text, life under an abbot in the cloister differs in degree but not in kind from life under a bishop in the world. To make too much of a distinction between monks on the one hand and Christian kings on the other or between Wilfrid's role as abbot and his role as bishop, would undermine the work's repeated emphasis upon the unconditional and universal character of God's call. In addition, although Stephen's *Life* is a work written by a monk and almost certainly for monks, it refuses to exalt the monastic life as the exclusive path toward virtue. In its modest way it displays the Christ type to its monastic audience more in the form of obedient kings like Alhfrith, Aethilred, and Caedwalla than in the form of virtuous monks. By so doing it shatters a monk's temptation both to view his own cloistered life as, *ipso facto*, the guarantor of Christlike humility and to view, conversely, the worldly life of kings as inherently inimical to that same end. Yet at the same time, it displays a suspicion of worldly power through portraits of kings like Ecgfrith and Aldfrith. Refusing to portray kings stereotypically as either one way or the other, Stephen forces the reader to quit trying to correlate titles of worldly status with status before God. To him, it matters little whether one is king, priest or monk. What really matters is whether one is willing to accept the divine call to sonship and to respond with a humility that manifests itself through obedience--obedience to spiritual fathers on earth who have received their authority to teach, to legislate, to bind and to loose from their Father who is in Heaven.

CHAPTER FOUR

A CLOUD OF WITNESSES--
WILFRID AND THE EARLY MEDIEVAL BISHOPS OF
ROME AND LYON

The last two chapters examined the way that Stephen the priest sought to portray Wilfrid's sanctity in his *Life of Bishop Wilfrid*. That examination revolved around two central images in Stephen's portrait: Wilfrid as apostle-prophet and Wilfrid as devoted father. So far, this study has considered Stephen's text and the world it presents. The question of whether Stephen's account of events accords well with that of other contemporary sources, that of Bede's *Ecclesiastical History*, for example, has not claimed our attention. That question is, strictly speaking, a historical one--historical, that is, in the sense defined in chapter one as *external history*, namely, history conceived as the objective and scientific reporting of facts and data. By contrast, the preceding chapters have been more concerned with *internal history*, that is, a history that concerns itself less with the so-called objective sequence of events and more with the admittedly subjective meaning which those events had for valuing human selves and their communities. Internal history raises questions about a person's or a community's religious convictions or about how they interpret the separate events of their particular lives as belonging to a larger, purposive, and ultimate unity. Unlike a catechism, Stephen's *Life of Wilfrid* does not answer such questions in a straightforward way. It chooses rather to answer them by telling Wilfrid's story from its own partial viewpoint.

Stephen saw Wilfrid as one in whom the power of God manifested itself in an exemplary way. He claims no absolute uniqueness for Wilfrid in this regard. In fact, he takes pains to show that God intervenes in Wilfrid's life in much the same way that God intervened in the lives of the Old Testament prophets, the New Testament apostles, and even Christ himself. Wilfrid is thus shown to imitate earlier types of Christ both in what he does and in what he experiences. Just as the biblical types were called by God, persecuted by men, and then glorified by God for their faith, so, according to Stephen, was Wilfrid.

The Quest for Wilfrid's Self-Understanding

Having considered in chapter two Stephen's understanding of Wilfrid in terms of the prophet-apostle type, the historian who is more interested in Wilfrid than in Stephen's characterization of him might begin to wonder how much Stephen's interpretation of Wilfrid's story would have agreed with the historical Wilfrid's interpretation of the same. Did Wilfrid notice the similarity between his and the apostles' experience? If so, did he share that insight with his abbots, monks, and priests? Since Wilfrid left no direct communication about how he understood the remarkable events of his life or his role in them, such questions will yield no certain answers. They may, however, yield some plausible hypotheses.

In this respect, the modern biographer of Wilfrid enjoys a greater prospect of success than biographers of many other ancient men and women. Some modern theologians and New Testament historians, for example, have abandoned hope of ever recovering Jesus' understanding of himself and his ministry--and with some reason.1 As noted in the first chapter, the author of the Gospel of Mark, the earliest Gospel, did not complete this life of Jesus until about forty years after Jesus' death and almost certainly did not participate as eyewitness in the events he described. By contrast, Stephen

1 For example, in responding to those who think it possible to recover the inner life of Jesus, Leander Keck writes: "The course of critical investigation since Herrmann has led to the opposite conclusion--that the inner life of Jesus is precisely what cannot be known" (196, n. 16).

wrote the *Life of Wilfrid* no later than six years after Wilfrid's death. He knew Wilfrid personally, having belonged to the first generation of Wilfrid's monastic *familia*, and was commissioned to compose the *Life* by two of Wilfrid's closest associates and companions, Abbots Tatberht of Ripon and Acca of Hexham.2 Given the close association that Stephen enjoyed with Wilfrid and with those who knew him most intimately, one would expect that the historical Wilfrid's own self-understanding influenced Stephen's literary portrayal of him.

And what a singular portrayal that is. A careful reading of the earliest Northumbrian saints' Lives reveals that the *Life of Wilfrid*'s view of sanctity differs substantially from that of the others, especially the two prose Lives of Cuthbert. Although Stephen twice copies verbatim the anonymous author's descriptions of Cuthbert and ascribes them to Wilfrid, his Wilfrid yet retains a stubborn uniqueness.3 For Stephen, teaching and subsequent persecution stand out as the identifying marks of the apostolic life as Wilfrid embodied it; for the anonymous author, asceticism and wonder-working emerge as Cuthbert's outstanding virtues.4 In his *Ecclesiastical History*, Bede portrays the sanctity of men like Aidan, Chad, and John of Beverley in roughly the same way that the anonymous monk of Lindisfarne portrays Cuthbert's sanctity, namely, in terms of their wonder-working power, extreme asceticism, or both.5 By saying less about Wilfrid's healing powers and asceticism, and choosing instead to stress Wilfrid's faithfulness to his call amidst persecution, Stephen clearly sets forth an atypical understanding of sanctity for early Christian Northumbria.

---

2 For the dating of Stephen's *Life*, see above, ch. 1, notes 1 and 16.

3 The LW Praefatio and LW ch. 11 duplicate long portions of the LCA Prologue and LCA 4.1, respectively.

4 These two different understandings of *imitatio apostolorum* can be seen already in the second and third centuries. As Karl S. Frank has shown, the earliest apocryphal apostolic *Acta* emphasize the wonder-working and ascetic qualities of the apostles and their imitators (153-156); yet these *Acta*, in much the same spirit as the writings of Origen and Eusebius, mark out pesecution and subsequent martyrdom as an essential part of the apostolic way (Frank 159, 163, 166).

5 Cf. Aidan: EH 3.5, 14-17; Chad: EH 4.3; John of Beverley: EH 5.2-6.

The uniqueness of Stephen's portrait must be owing to one or more of the following: (1) Stephen's highly personal and idiosyncratic viewpoint, (2) the common viewpoint of Wilfrid's monastic *familia*, or (3) Wilfrid's own viewpoint. The second possibility seems far more likely than the first. Since Ripon's Abbot Tatberht and Hexham's Bishop Acca commissioned Stephen to write the *Life*, the resulting work has more the character of an official biography than of Stephen's personal reminiscences. It must reflect the view of Wilfrid's entire monastic and clerical *familia*. Yet the *familia*'s peculiar way of viewing the significance of their "father" may reflect the peculiarity of the "father" himself--the peculiarity of his life experiences, personality, training, and self- understanding as bishop and abbot. Most directly, therefore, Stephen's *Life* probably drew its inspiration from the corporate memory of Wilfrid's spiritual *familia*. Indirectly, Wilfrid himself put his stamp upon it.

The same might be said of Cuthbert's influence on his *Lives*. Behind the divergent hagiographical portraits of Cuthbert and Wilfrid, therefore, there lurks the existence of two equally divergent historical personalities whose common background might have been expected to have given them more in common than it apparently did. Both were born in about 634, both were Anglo-Saxon, both lived under the monastic regimen at Lindisfarne, and both ruled as bishops in their native Northumbria. Yet despite these similarities, one critical factor in Wilfrid's biography sets him apart both from Cuthbert and from many of his other contemporaries in the Northumbrian church: his first pilgrimage to Rome.6 In one of the most illuminating pieces ever written on Wilfrid, Henry Mayr-Harting stresses Wilfrid's Continental contacts as crucial to the development of his episcopal style (129-147). Wilfrid made those contacts during that first pilgrimage to Rome, which began when he was about eighteen and lasted perhaps six or seven years.7

---

6 The exception to this rule is Benedict Biscop, founder of Wearmouth-Jarrow monastery, who journeyed to Rome several times (EH 4.18, LW ch. 3, and LA chs. 2, 4, 6 and 9).

7 Stephen states that on his way to Rome Wilfrid spent a year in Kent (ch. 3) and that on his way back he spent three years in Lyon (ch. 6). Although this information accounts for four years of Wilfrid's journey, it remains to be known how long Wilfrid actually stayed in Rome itself or how long he spent in Lyon on the first leg of his journey.

Besides Rome, Wilfrid also visited Lyon for three years on his return trip home. In both of these great ancient Christian sees, Wilfrid encountered an ecclesiastical culture far different from that of Northumbria. The church in each city boasted a tradition of famous, powerful bishops and a thriving cult of local martyrs.

Mayr-Harting convincingly shows how Wilfrid's anomalous style of episcopal leadership in Northumbria would have hardly raised an eyebrow in seventh-century Gaul, especially Lyon. He concludes that Wilfrid learned how to be bishop by observing and remembering Gallic examples, including the example of his alleged mentor, Archbishop Annemundus of Lyon (130-139). That style roughly corresponds to the fatherly traits that Stephen ascribes to Wilfrid, as discussed in the previous chapter. Drawing upon Mayr-Harting's insight, the present chapter asks whether and to what extent the historical Wilfrid encountered on his first pilgrimage to Rome the two types that Stephen portrays him as imitating: the persecuted prophet-apostle and the spiritual father.

If Wilfrid observed the bishops of Rome and Lyon embodying these two types, he first did so, it must be noted, while participating in the Christian rite of pilgrimage. As historians of religions and cultural anthropologists have argued, the ritual participant experiences the world of ritual as sacred. Its time, place, and action are felt to be infused with a sacrality rarely experienced in mundane, everyday life (Eliade 35). As religious ritual, pilgrimage has an important initiatory function.8 During its course, the initiate migrates from the mundane center of his or her everyday world to a sacred periphery, partakes of the mystery and transformative power associated with this periphery, and then returns to the everyday world as one who has been enlightened.

Once the historian grows to appreciate pilgrimage's deeply affective dimension as a rite of passage, Wilfrid's first journey to Rome and Lyon takes on greater significance than even Mayr-Harting ascribed to it. Not only would the pilgrimage equip Wilfrid with valuable training for his eventual vocation as abbot and bishop, it would also implant the idea of the vocation

---

8 The classic pioneering study is by van Gennep. On pilgrimage as a rite of passage, see the following by Victor Turner: *Dramas* 166-271, *Process* 143-153, and *Image* 6-18.

itself and instill the conviction that God had specially singled him out for it. If Wilfrid had been only toying with the idea of an ecclesiastical career before leaving for Rome, he surely had it firmly in mind by the time he got back. If he had regarded men like Aidan and Finan as the highest examples of sanctity and episcopal virtue, he would regard them no longer as such once his pilgrimage was done. Having left the mundane center of his native Northumbria and made pilgrimage to the sacred periphery, to the faraway sees of Rome and Lyon, Wilfrid underwent a dramatic conversion. For that sacred periphery eventually formed the center of Wilfrid's piety, while the old mundane center, populated as it was with old ascetic heroes like Aidan, retreated more and more to the periphery of his self-definition as bishop and abbot.

Wilfrid and the Martyr Type in Rome and Lyon

As the second chapter has already shown, Stephen lays particular stress on persecution at the hands of hostile human agents as a distinguishing mark of the prophet-apostle type. Although persecution plays a central role in Stephen's *Life of Wilfrid*, the earliest hagiographical narratives of other Northumbrian bishops such as Aidan, Chad, Cuthbert, and John of Beverley never mention it at all. Persecution functions for Stephen as the specific mode of Christlike suffering which Wilfrid's life exemplifies. Just because these other holy men did not experience Christlike suffering in the form of persecution is not to say that they did not experience suffering at all. As men whom their hagiographers venerated as types of Christ, they were recognized as having a different kind of cross to bear.

By the seventh century, the Christian imagination came to recognize several forms of suffering as Christlike. In order to help distinguish among those several forms, the early medieval imagination offered several systems of classification which associated the several forms of Christlike suffering with certain types of martyrdom. For example, a seventh-century Irish text distinguishes among red martyrdom, which signifies dying for the sake of

Christ, and two other non-bloody forms of martyrdom: white and green.9
For present purposes, we shall adopt the terminology of Pope Gregory the
Great, who designates bloody suffering as public martyrdom, and non-bloody
suffering as secret martyrdom. According to Gregory, public martyrdom,
which ends in bodily death, occurs during times of persecution; secret
martyrdom occurs when persecution has ceased. For Gregory, however, the
secret martyrs are no less admirable than the public ones, for "Did they not
[also] endure the assaults of a hidden enemy? Did they not love their
enemies in this world? Did they not resist every carnal desire? By sacrificing
themselves in this way to almighty God on the altar of their hearts they
became true martyrs, even in times of peace" (*Dialogues* 3.26; cf. Rush).
Gregory included among the secret martyrs those monastic heroes who
suffered deprivation and tribulation in their bodies every day, though not in
the form of human persecutors. Aidan, Cuthbert, and Chad belong in this
category. Wilfrid, however, must be placed in the other.

If Stephen's depiction of Wilfrid derives from Wilfrid's own self-
understanding, one wonders how Wilfrid alone of all the early bishops of
Northumbria came to imitate the type of the persecuted, public martyr. As a
youth at Lindisfarne, Wilfrid would have personally witnessed no living
examples of the public martyr. As part of Iona's Christian tradition,
Lindisfarne could hold up for him a proud heritage of ascetic saints and
pilgrims, but comparatively few martyrs. That being so, where might Wilfrid
have encountered the ideal of the public martyr to such an extent that it
would stimulate his piety and inform his self-understanding as a man of God?

---

9 Stokes 2:246-247:

> Now there are three kinds of martyrdom which are counted as a
> cross to man, that is to say, white martyrdom, and green martyrdom, and red
> martyrdom.
> This is the white martyrdom to man, when he separates for sake of
> God from everything he loves, although he suffers fasting or labour thereat.
> This is the green martyrdom to him, when by means of them [i.e.,
> fasting and labour] he separates from his desires, or suffers toil in penance
> and repentance.
> This is red martyrdom to him, endurance of a cross or destruction
> for Christ's sake as happened to the apostles in the persecution of the wicked
> and in teaching the law of God.

The most obvious answer is Rome and Lyon, the two cities that Stephen specially mentions in conjunction with Wilfrid's first pilgrimage (LW chs. 4-6). As two of the most ancient sees in the western church, Rome and Lyon boasted a proud tradition of martyrs who suffered during the pre-Constantinian age.

Rome had long been regarded as the pre-eminent church of the martyrs. Its privilege of honor in the early church had derived largely from its double apostolic foundation upon Sts. Peter and Paul. As early as the late third century, Tertullian can write of Rome:

> How happy is its church, on which the apostles poured forth all their doctrine along with their blood! where Peter endures a passion like his Lord's! where Paul wins his crown in a death like John's [i.e., the Baptist's]! where the Apostle John was first plunged unhurt, into boiling oil, and thence remitted to his island-exile. (*On Prescription Against Heretics* ch. 36)

Clearly for Tertullian, Rome's primacy of honor derives from the apostolic teaching and suffering which happened there. The deaths of these apostles, however, only began Rome's rich tradition of martyrs. That tradition continued with the martyrs who suffered during the persecutions of Decius and Valerius (249-259 C.E.) and Diocletian (303-312 C.E.).[10]

In his narration of Wilfrid's first stay in Rome (ca. 654/655), Stephen states that Wilfrid daily circumnavigated the *limina martyrum* for many months in order to pray at martyrs' shrines (LW ch. 5). Virtually all of those shrines had been erected in honor of public rather than secret martyrs, and that despite Gregory the Great's assertion of their equality. These shrines included some new and impressive ones. Only seventy years old would have been the basilica enclosing the grave of St. Laurence, built by Pope Pelagius II (579-590). Even newer were the impressive churches that Pope Honorius built in about 630, one over the tomb of the martyred St. Agnes, the other over St. Pancras (Krautheimer 85-86). Such are only three of the countless *martyria* which Wilfrid likely visited.

---

10 For more on the persecutions under Decius and Valerius, and Diocletian, see Frend 285-325 and 351-392.

In addition to the martyrs' physical remains, Wilfrid would have heard stories of their passions. Not to be hindered by a lack of historical detail, Roman hagiographers of the fifth and sixth centuries had freely created legends about Rome's most celebrated martyrs, including those of Sts. Sebastian, Cecile, Domitilla, Martina, Calocerus and Parthenius, Abandius and Abundantius, and Eusebius and Pontian.11 Traveling from shrine to shrine, perhaps with the aid of such guidebooks as seventh-century pilgrims in Rome were known to have used, Wilfrid would have recalled the story of each martyrs' *passio* as he visited his or her shrine.12

Like Rome, the church of Lyon could boast a rich tradition of martyrs, especially in its early period. In his *Ecclesiastical History* Eusebius records a letter from the early Lyon church that tells the story of those heroic martyrs of Lyon who, during the Aurelian persecution (ca. 177 C.E.), endured every conceivable kind of torture in the Lyon amphitheatre (5.1). Martyred with them was Lyon's bishop Pothinus. Though ninety years old and physically weak, he was nevertheless "strengthened by zeal of spirit through the urgent desire of martyrdom" (5.1.29). Battered and beaten, he died two days later in prison. According to Gregory of Tours' doubtful authority, the famous anti-Gnostic Irenaeus succeeded Pothinus as bishop and also died a martyr (*History of the Franks* 1.29).

After Constantine granted Christians legal recognition in 313, the ideal of martyrdom became spiritualized and monasticized in Lyon as it had elsewhere.13 The new ascetic ideal did not, however, displace the martyr.

---

11 For more on the nature and historical veracity of these early medieval Roman *passiones*, see Delehaye, "L'Amphitheatre Flavien."

12 Two such pilgrim guidebooks have been reprinted in De Rossi, *La Roma sotterranea* 138-143. For more on the phenomenon of early medieval pilgrimage to Rome, see Colgrave, "Pilgrimages."

13 By the time Wilfrid arrived in Lyon, it had already become the breeding ground for two ascetic traditions. The first, associated with Lérins, had grown up on Gallo-Roman soil and had given Lyon such saintly ascetic bishops as Justus (d. 390), Eucherius (d. 449), and Lupus (d. 542). The second, often called the Hiberno-Frankish tradition, had been more recently propagated by St. Columbanus (d. 615). For more on these two traditions see Prinz, *Frühes Mönchtum* 47-76 and 121-151. Additional material on the Hiberno-Frankish tradition is in Clarke.

Churches dedicated to the public martyrs of an earlier era still dotted Lyon's early medieval ecclesiastical landscape. Its cathedral church bore the name of St. Stephen, the protomartyr, while two other major churches were dedicated to the Maccabean Martyrs and to the Apostles and the Forty-Eight Martyrs. Within these churches rested the remains of Lyon's great martyrs, including those of Irenaeus and the martyrs of Aurelian persecution.14 Gregory of Tours relates that in one of these churches, the dust that rested on the martyrs tombs was infused with a special healing power (*Liber in gloria martyrum* ch. 48). If Wilfrid prayed daily at the martyrs' shrines in Rome during his several months there, he may have continued that practice during his three years in Lyon.

It takes little imagination to envision just how great a spiritual impact the martyrs' shrines and churches in Rome and Lyon would have made on a young Anglo-Saxon like Wilfrid. Yet even more dramatic than his encounter with the martyrs' heritage in each of these two cities would have been his encounter with actual martyrdoms that were taking place during his visits there. In attempting to account for Wilfrid's later behavior as bishop in England, no scholar of Wilfrid appears to have noticed the significance of what was happening in these two cities when Wilfrid first visited them. Yet such an observation may be crucial for understanding why Wilfrid, as bishop, seemed to approximate the self-consciousness of a public martyr rather than that of the ascetic.

Were a history of martyrdom in Rome and Lyon during the four centuries after Constantine to be written, a slim volume would result. Between the time that Christianity gained toleration from Constantine in 313 and the beginning of the eighth century, only one pope and one archbishop of Lyon were venerated as martyrs. The pope, Martin I, died in exile in September 655 and the archbishop of Lyon, Annemundus, was murdered three years later in about 658.15 It would have been amazing enough had

---

14 For more on the church of St. Stephen and the other Lyon churches during the early medieval period, see Coville 441-469 and Ewig, "Kirche und Civitas" 8-10.

15 Silverius (536-537) also came to be venerated as a martyr, but not until the eleventh century (Kelly 60). For the life and martyrdom of Annemundus, see the *Acta [sancti Annemundi]*.

Wilfrid encountered only one of these martyrdoms on his pilgrimage, but in fact he encountered them both, happening to be in the right place at the right time to witness some events in the dramas of both. When examining the story of each martyrdom--always keeping Wilfrid's later career in mind--one can hardly help noticing not only that these two bishops seemed to court persecution, but that they bore the wrath of secular officials for the same reasons that Wilfrid later would. A more thorough examination of these parallels requires relating the story behind each of these martyrdoms as Wilfrid might have seen them.

Wilfrid arrived in Rome in about 654 and left perhaps sometime in 655 (Plummer 316-317). Scarcely could he have picked a more tumultuous time for his visit. On Saturday, June 15, 653--scarcely a year before Wilfrid's arrival--the imperial exarch and the Ravenna army had marched into Rome. By Monday, they had stormed the basilica of the Lateran palace and seized a severely ill Pope Martin. By Tuesday, they spirited Martin away under cover of night and took him by sea to Constantinople for trial. After a miserable three-month voyage, Martin was imprisoned for three more months, tried and found guilty of treason against the emperor, and exiled to the Crimea where for the next year-and-a-half he suffered from cold, shortage of food, and harsh conditions. Death mercifully greeted him on September 16, 655.16

What had Pope Martin done to merit such treatment? Like several of his recent predecessors, he had refused to compromise with the emperor on Christological issues. The early seventh-century emperors had more of a political than a religious interest in Christology. Threatened from the south and east by Arab and Persian invaders, they needed all of the military and political support they could muster, including that of the heretical Monophysites, who affirmed against the Chalcedonian settlement that Christ had only a single divine nature.17 In an attempt to win support from the

---

16 The story of Martin's abduction, trial, exile, and death can be pieced together through the following sources: LP ch. 76 (Martin); Martin, *Epp.* 14-17 in PL 87.197-204.; and Anastasius, *Collectanea*, "Commemoratio eorum quae...acta sunt...in...Martinum papam," in PL 129.591-604.

17 For the relationship of the East's political, military, and theological problems, see Bury 391-403.

Monophysites, imperial policy since 638 had promoted the compromise doctrine of Monotheletism, which affirmed that if Christ had two natures, he at least had a single divine will (Bury 398). In the midst of these imperial attempts at conciliation, Martin convened 105 bishops in the Lateran synod of 649.18 Under Martin's papal leadership, the synod condemned Monotheletism and thus undermined the emperor's attempts to win Monophysite support in the East. The emperor, understandably enraged, sought revenge against Martin for his role in the synod. Unable to punish the pope on religious grounds, the emperor had his agents in Italy fabricate the treason charge that resulted in Martin's abduction, trial, exile and death.

By all accounts, mid-seventh-century Roman clergy and citizens cared as much as Martin did about preserving Roman orthodoxy and resisting the emperor's attempts to compromise Rome's doctrinal purity. The matter to them was one both of principle and, in time, of civic pride.19 Imperial maltreatment of Pope Martin revealed to mid-seventh-century Romans nothing that they had not seen before and would not see again: five years before Martin's abduction, imperial forces had exiled the papal *apocrisarios* in Constantinople for refusing to subscribe to *Typos*, the imperial decree that suspended all Christological debate;20 shortly after Martin's abduction, the imperial army entered Rome again, this time to nab the intellectual leader of orthodox forces, the old Greek-speaking Abbot Maximus. Like Martin, Maximus was taken to Constantinople, tried for treason, and exiled. Later his tongue and right hand were cut off. By virtue of his torments and his eloquent defense of Chalcedonian orthodoxy he has become known to

---

18 For a more detailed account of the synod, see Riedinger.

19 Just how much the citizens of Rome cared about Christological issues and the primacy of Rome's church can be seen in the fact that they held Martin's successor to the papacy, Eugenius, captive in his church until he agreed to reject the synodical letter of Peter, the new Monothelete patriarch of Constantinople. See LP ch. 77 and Richards 192.

20 Richards 186. For an abridged translation of *Typos*, see Hefele 5:95-96. The complete text is in Mansi 10:1029.

posterity as Maximus the Confessor.21

Wilfrid doubtless knew of the treatment that the *apocrisarios*, Pope Martin, and Maximus had received at the emperor's hands and may have even arrived at Rome in time to see imperial troops arrest Maximus. He also would have known that all three men were suffering for their refusal to capitulate to imperial demands in matters of doctrine and canon law. If Stephen's and Bede's narratives are to be believed, an older Bishop Wilfrid would prove himself to be as stalwart against Northumbrian kings Ecgfrith and Aldfrith as Martin and Maximus had once been against the emperor. Like Martin and Maximus, Wilfrid refused to tailor church custom and discipline to the needs or whims of secular powers. Later in life, whenever Wilfrid brought suit against the Northumbrian kings who had despoiled him of his see, he always based his case on the fact that the actions they had taken against him had no canonical precedent and so contravened established ecclesiastical norms and discipline.22 The Northumbrian kings, however, were as deaf to Wilfrid's arguments as the emperor was to Martin's.

Martin's courage exemplified the bravado of his immediate predecessors in the Roman See. In the 640s papal rule had proved itself stubbornly immune to imperial bullying. Pope John IV (640-642), for example, rejected *Ekthesis*, the imperial edict which promulgated Monotheletism, and Pope Theodore (642-649) excommunicated the acting patriarch of Constantinople. Neither action pleased the emperor.23 Learning from the example of these fearless popes, Wilfrid the bishop would later play out a similar drama in relationship to the powers and principalities

---

21 The story of Maximus' trials are chronicled in Anastasius, *Collectanea*, "Relatio motionis factae inter domnum abbatem Maximum et socium eius atque principes in secretario," in PL 129:603-624.

22 On separate occasions, the Northumbrian kings Ecgfrith (671-685) and Aldfrith (685-705) exiled Wilfrid and deposed him from his see. Both times Wilfrid complains that the actions taken against him violated ecclesiastical canons. Throughout Stephen's *Life*, Wilfrid is continually depicted as one who views the injustices done to him largely in terms of the violation of well-defined canonical norms and procedures. Cf. LW chs. 17, 29, 30, 41, 43, 45, and 46.

23 For more on the actions of Popes John IV (640-642) and Theodore I (642-649), see Richards 183-186. See also their separate entries in LP chs. 74 and 75, respectively.

of his world as the bishops of Rome of the 640s and 50s had done in their world. Having seen or heard rumor of their courageous example, he duplicated in himself their dangerous style of episcopal leadership and suffered long years of exile as a result, just as Pope Martin and the abbot Maximus had.

If Wilfrid had returned directly to England after leaving Rome, the images of Rome's first martyr, St. Peter, and Rome's latest martyr-bishop, Pope Martin, would have made a deep impression upon him by themselves. Yet the pilgrim Wilfrid's encounter with martyred bishops had only begun. It would require a three-year stay in Lyon for its completion.

Stephen gives a more complete account of Wilfrid's time in Lyon than in Rome and does so by focusing almost exclusively upon Wilfrid's relationship with Lyon's Archbishop Annemundus. If Stephen's *Life* had survived as the only source for Annemundus' life, Annemundus would be remembered simply as Wilfrid's doting spiritual father: ever pastoral, ever meek, ever gentle (LW chs. 4 and 6). The other narrative source that does survive, however, offers quite another side to the archbishop's personality and pastoral style. It is the *Acta sancti Annemundi*, a Frankish source which in its original redaction probably dates back to the eighth century (Coville 375). In it we see an immensely powerful archbishop who sometimes inspired trust, sometimes suspicion in the kings and princes of his own and neighboring territories. However kindly Annemundus may have acted toward Wilfrid, Annemundus' *Acta* states that he wielded such powers of intimidation that few nobles in the royal assembly dared disagree with him openly and that, as a result, he "met with hatred in all of them" (ch. 2). Smoldering thus with resentment, certain nobles accused him of using his role as godfather and counsellor to the boy-king Clotar III in order to seize royal power for himself. Their accusations soon reached the ears of a worried Frankish Queen Balthild, the young Clotar's mother, so that she summoned Annemundus for questioning. One night, as Annemundus was making his way to the tribunal, two men with swords murdered him in his tent (AsA chs. 10-11). Despite the many uncertainties surrounding Annemundus' martyrdom, his death seems to have resulted from a newly developing power-struggle in Burgundian Gaul between at least two factions.

On one side were churchmen like Annemundus who jealously guarded the traditional authority and privileges of the old Gallo-Roman church and episcopate; on the other was a coalition composed of Queen Balthild, members of the new Frankish aristocracy, and representatives of the new Columbanan monasticism. Together, though probably for different reasons, these three groups were hoping to diminish and decentralize traditional Gallo-Roman episcopal power.24

Stephen reports that Wilfrid wanted to suffer martyrdom with Annemundus, but that because he was Anglo-Saxon, the Frankish executioners spared his life (LW ch. 6). From the point of view of external history, Stephen's narration of this episode has been regarded as suspect.25 Nevertheless, the general impression that it conveys of a Wilfrid ready and willing to do battle with secular authorities, even if that meant exile or martyrdom, rings so true to episodes in his later life as bishop that we must accord that narrative some credence as providing at least an ideal image by which Wilfrid understood himself and others remembered him.

The four to six years between Wilfrid's arrival home and his episcopal consecration gave him ample time to reflect upon what he had witnessed during his five-year-long pilgrimage. Etched in his memory and imagination, to be sure, were the shrines and relics of the ancient martyrs that he had especially gone to see. More impressive, however, must have been the examples of contemporary martyrdoms that Wilfrid either witnessed or about which he heard. In both Martin and Annemundus, Wilfrid encountered examples of powerful bishops who, like the prophets, apostles, and martyred bishops of old, suffered death for the church's faith at the hands of worldly powers and principalities. From the likes of both bishops, Wilfrid learned

---

24 For a fuller account on the new situation faced by Gallic bishops in the seventh and eighth centuries, see Ewig, "Milo" 207-219. Prinz argues that the Columbanan monastic establishment was strongly opposed to the kind of ecclesiastical-state that old Gallo-Roman styled bishops like Annemundus were intent on building and maintaining (*Frühes Mönchtum* 176).

25 Janet Nelson has concluded from her chronological investigations that Wilfrid was already home in England when Annemundus was martyred (66).

how to rule with authority and how to endure humiliation when that authority aroused the envy of secular rulers.

Wilfrid did not die as a martyr, as did the apostles and bishops whom he most admired. He did, however, share in their experience of being persecuted. In chapter six, Stephen claims that Wilfrid's brush with death in Gaul earned him the status of confessor, that is, one who suffered grave danger as a testimony to the faith but who did not die as a consequence (LW ch. 6). Whether or not Stephen's account of this episode is historically accurate, the picture that it leaves of Wilfrid as one who courageously confronts secular authority accords well with what is known about Bishop Wilfrid's later relations with the Northumbrian kings Ecgfrith and Aldfrith. As a bishop he lived dangerously, taking stands and performing actions which might have been predicted to provoke royal wrath. For example, by taking so long to return from his episcopal consecration in Gaul, Wilfrid likely tried the patience of King Oswiu, who in exasperation consecrated Chad in the Northumbrian see already designated for Wilfrid. Or again, by seeming to aid and abet Queen Aethelthryth in her desire to remain a virgin, Wilfrid turned King Ecgfrith into an implacable enemy (EH 4.19; cf. Foley, "Imitatio" 24-28). And finally, by appealing his case against Kings Ecgfrith and Aldfrith to Rome, Wilfrid probably embarrassed them as much as he enlightened them. He thus increased the likelihood of their continuing to persecute him.

Unless Wilfrid naively miscalculated these royal reactions to his behavior, one must conclude that he did not act as he did simply to achieve his personal ends, for those ends could have been achieved had he behaved in a craftier and more politic way. By acting so uncompromisingly, stubbornly, and in ways that, from one perspective, doomed his episcopal career in Northumbria to failure, Wilfrid showed his true colors as a subversive. For besides shipwrecking his own career, his actions powerfully subverted all-too-common royal assumptions about the proper relation between earthly and heavenly authority. Whereas the kings saw that relation in terms of easy alliance, Wilfrid seems to have seen it instead in terms of radical obedience, obedience owed from kings, no less than monks, to God. For Wilfrid, willingness to submit to the discipline and doctrine that God had entrusted successively to Christ, the apostles, and the Roman church served as the litmus test of that obedience.

During the Christological controversy of the seventh century, emperors at Constantinople twice had attempted to force the Roman church to compromise on doctrinal issues whose extreme volatility was threatening the Eastern empire's survival. In 634 the Constantinopolitan patriarch Sergius, acting as the emperor's agent, proposed to Pope Honorius I the compromise doctrine of Monothelitism (Bury 399). Although Honorius himself was willing to wink at this new doctrine, the Roman church roundly rejected it after his death and condemned his memory for even appearing to accept it. Hoping again for a compromise and realizing that he would never get the Roman church to make peace with the Monophysites, Emperor Constans II issued the edict *Typos* in 648. In *Typos* Constans ordered all Christological discussion to cease, hoping that at least by silencing the debate he might win back some Monophysite support. The Roman church, however, also roundly rejected *Typos* at the Lateran synod in 649.

During his first pilgrimage in the early 650s, Wilfrid would have seen a Roman church unwilling to yield--or even give the appearance of yielding-- to imperial demands. He thus learned from his Roman teachers that the church has its own divinely entrusted prerogatives which it will let the temporal powers abrogate only at its peril. Such teachers taught him by example perhaps more than by word. Having either witnessed or heard report of Pope Martin's and Maximus' recent tribulations, Wilfrid came to know full well the awful price that an obedient, God-fearing saint might be called upon to pay. By the time Wilfrid became bishop of Northumbria in 664, he had learned well that the church that found its unity in Rome's apostolic authority had always been willing to sacrifice and suffer. To suffer thus at the hands of the secular ruler befell no early Northumbrian bishop except Wilfrid. Yet however singular his trials seemed to some, Wilfrid knew that those trials replicated the experiences of all of God's chosen, whether they had lived in the olden days--as had the prophets, apostles, and early bishop-martyrs of Rome and Lyon--or in more recent times, as had Pope Martin, Maximus the Confessor, and Archbishop Annemundus.

Wilfrid and the *Pius-Pater* Type in Rome and Lyon

As chapter three shows, the Wilfrid who in Stephen's *Life* suffered persecution along with the prophets, apostles, and early Christian martyrs also experienced God's glorification. For upon him were conferred the powerful fatherly offices of bishop and abbot, not to mention a potent personal charisma. To depict Wilfrid in this way serves Stephen's larger theological and apologetical ends, but does it do justice to the way that the historical Wilfrid understood his fatherly authority? Like his depiction of Wilfrid-the-persecuted, Stephen's depiction of Wilfrid-the-powerful-father appears as an anomaly when compared to the earliest images of other Northumbrian bishops like Aidan, Cuthbert, and Chad. Wilfrid's episcopal power threatens kings; Aidan's and Cuthbert's endears kings to them. Wilfrid ever applies himself to enforcing universally the canons and the discipline taught in Rome; Cuthbert and Chad, though not hostile to such canons, exhibit little interest in such matters.26 Wilfrid moves in a world of royal and episcopal courts, always accompanied by a band of loyal followers; Cuthbert moves alone in a world of peasants and small Northumbrian villages.

Like his picture of Wilfrid-the-persecuted, Stephen's picture of Wilfrid-the-Father probably grew out of Wilfrid's own understanding of the privileges and duties that go with the bishop's office. That understanding, like his understanding of obedient discipleship, probably depended heavily upon the examples he observed in Rome and Lyon during his first pilgrimage. Just as he looked to the continent for his episcopal consecration in 664, so would he have looked to the continent throughout the rest of his life to provide him with an episcopal ideal to imitate in the daily execution of his office (LW ch. 12). The rest of this chapter seeks to uncover that ideal as Wilfrid would have encountered it during his first pilgrimage to the continent, and especially in Rome and Lyon. Like the type of the bishop-

---

26 There is one exception here. Bede depicts Cuthbert in one place as exhorting the monks of Lindisfarne to learn the catholic statutes of the fathers and to practice the institutes of the regular life (LCP ch. 39). This characterization of Cuthbert is absent in the earlier *Anonymous Life of St. Cuthbert*. It may be that Bede's depiction of Cuthbert as concerned with such matters was influenced by Stephen's similar depiction of Wilfrid.

martyr, the type of the bishop-father became known to him both generally, through the Latin tradition of episcopal leadership, and specifically, through his own eyewitness experience of particular bishops and the legacy of recent bishops in both Rome and Lyon.

Development of Episcopal Authority in the West since the Fourth Century: A Brief Overview

Chapter three demonstrated that the title of *father* became applied to the bishop more frequently as the history of the early church progressed. With Constantine's accession in 312 C.E., bishops acquired new powers of legal jurisdiction and augmented their fatherly authority by assuming the duties of judge.27 Constantine's removal of the imperial capital from Rome to Constantinople contributed even more to the bishop's power in the West. Rome and the great Roman cities of Gaul, once ruled by their civic *curiae*, came increasingly under episcopal control. No strangers to the world of status and might, these bishops came as often as not from old Roman and Gallo-Roman aristocratic families that had recently converted to Christianity.28 The immense power that these bishops wielded also owed much to their individual initiative. Asserting his fatherly authority both in theory and practice, Archbishop Ambrose of Milan (339-397), for example, likens the bishop to a *paterfamilias* who rules over his servant-sons in the same way that God rules as father over his servant-son, the bishop.29 In Ambrose's mind, the bishop properly exercised his spiritual authority over

---

27 In 321 C.E., for example, bishops received power to manumit slaves, a privilege that had been reserved for provincial governors. Constantine also decreed that either party could transfer a lawsuit to the authority of the local bishop if dissatisfied with the local civil court at any stage of the trial. This decree alone immersed the bishop in affairs of state, thus establishing him as an important secular as well as spiritual figure. The bishop's role as judge assumed even greater significance during the fifth century when the bishop took on certain civic duties that the imperial *defensor civitatis* and the *curator operum publicorum* had once shouldered (Jones 45, 90-91).

28 Pope Leo the Great, Bishop Ambrose of Milan, and Archbishop Eucherius of Lyon, for example, all came from distinguished Roman aristocratic families.

29 Ambrose *Ep.* 2.31 (ad Constantium episcopum), in PL 16.925-926: "Paterfamilias enim dicitur, ut quasi filios regat; quoniam et ipse Dei servus est, et patrem appellat Dominum coeli, moderatorem potestatum omnium."

Praetorian prefects, clergy, and laity. He regarded them all as his spiritual "sons."30

As Ambrose had done in the late fourth century, the bishops of Rome in the late fifth increasingly stressed their fatherly authority over the emperor. Papal fears that the emperors would try to win back Monophysite loyalists by compromising the Chalcedonian settlement called forth from Pope Gelasius I (492-496) a bold new statement defining where imperial *potestas* ended and priestly *auctoritas* began. Accepting as axiomatic that authority should be commensurate with responsibility, Gelasius reasoned that since God has singled out the priestly order as responsible on earth for oversight of matters spiritual, then final authority in those matters should be given to that order, especially to the bishops and most especially to the pope. In matters of ecclesiastical discipline and doctrine, therefore, bishops should teach, emperors learn.31

Gallic bishops of the same period exercised fatherly authority with equal or greater vigor than their Italian counterparts. These bishops have become justly famous for attending to every aspect of their flocks' welfare, physical as well as spiritual: when famine hit Burgundy, Lyon's Archbishop Patiens (456-498) fed thousands at his own expense; Bishop Desiderius of

---

30 In the closing sentence of a letter to the Praetorian prefect Titianus, Ambrose writes, "Love me as a son [loves his parent], for I love you as a parent [loves his son]" (*Ep.* 52.2 [ad Titianum], PL 16.1215: "Vale, et nos dilige, ut filius; quia nos te, ut parentes, diligimus"). He also regarded emperors as sons, and imagined that they regarded him as father. In a letter to Emperor Theodosius he mourned the death of Emperor Valentinian II and told with joy how Valentinian, though once Ambrose's enemy, came in time to esteem him as his father (*Ep.* 53.2 [ad Theodosium imperatorem], PL 16.1165-66: "atque tanto in me incubuerat affectu, ut quem ante persequebatur, nunc diligeret: quem ante ut adversarium repellebat, nunc ut parentem putaret").

31 Pope Felix III, *Ep.* 8.5 in Thiel 250: "Certum est enim, hoc rebus vestris esse salutare, ut quum de causis Dei agitur, et juxta ipsius constitutm regiam voluntatem secerdotibus Christi studeatis subdere, non praeferre, et sacrosancta per eorum praesules *discere* potius quam *docere*..." (emphasis added). It is widely believed that this letter was drafted for Pope Felix by his trusted archdeacon Gelasius, who succeeded Felix in the papacy (Kelly 48 and Jalland 319). For more on the Gelasian theory of papal power, see Ullmann 15-31, esp. 19.

Cahors (630-655) oversaw the building of the aqueducts.32 From a study of episcopal epitaphs from the fourth to seventh centuries, historian Martin Heinzelmann has identified particular episcopal virtues that early medieval Gaul prized most highly. He concludes that the most central is the ability to exercise power in a just, kind, and solicitous way. More than any other metaphor, that of father was employed to describe this kind of power, hence the frequent recurrence in these epitaphs of phrases like *amore pater, pater pietate*, and *pater populi*. Heinzelmann includes all of these labels under the general rubric of *pius pater* (152-158, 239). By this standard Gallic bishops were judged. To it, one may suppose, they aspired.

Although an episcopal epitaph might extol several different virtues, all were seen to grow out of a more fundamental fatherly *pietas*.33 Of them, *eloquentia* merits special mention. Drawing its power from the residual force of old Roman aristocratic tradition, *eloquentia* appears to be a virtue that the Gallic epitaphs reserve exclusively for bishops (126, 239-240). This fact underscores the central importance ascribed to a bishop's teaching and preaching, both of which derived their power from his *eloquentia*.34 As chapter three showed, Stephen described Wilfrid's fatherly qualities mostly in terms of Wilfrid's various teaching and preaching activities on the one hand and his role as fatherly protector and provider on the other. With Stephen, the composers of Gallic episcopal epitaphs praised a bishop on the one hand

---

32 On Patiens, see Sidonius Apollinaris Ep. 6.12, MGH AA: 8:801-802; on Desiderius, see Ep. 13 (to Bishop Caesarius) in PL 87.255. Works that discuss the Gallic bishops' immense power, both worldly and spiritual, include: Ewig, "Milo"; Prinz, "Die bischöfliche Stadtherrschaft"; and, to a lesser extent, Heinzelmann. For an opposing viewpoint, see Durliat, who insists that in matters temporal Gallic episcopal power was exercised strictly under the authority of the Merovingian kings.

33 Such virtues included *iustitia, integritas* and *moderatio*. See Heinzelmann 239-242.

34 By the beginning of the early Middle Ages, the notion of *eloquentia* had undergone great changes under the influence of the church's aversion to pagan learning. Stripped from *eloquentia* was the rhetor's old penchant for artful, flowery elegance of speech. The stress on being able to speak convincingly and with authority, however, remained. Augustine of Hippo advocated eloquence in Christian teaching and preaching. He recognized that rhetorical skill was itself theologically neutral. Teachers of truth might use it, but also might teachers of falsehood. Christian teachers should not, therefore, cultivate eloquence as an end in itself, but as an aid to Christian preaching. See OCD ch. 4.

for defending and giving alms to the poor and the weak and, on the other, for
castigating those nobles who took advantage of the weak (Heinzelmann 123-
129, 241; Prinz, "Die bischöfliche Stadtherrschaft" 4). The Gallic bishop
mediated and settled conflicts, a task which required legal and juristic
competence. Such competence fell fully within the range of his fatherly
attributes.

With some exceptions, these virtues which early medieval Gaul
admired in its bishops, Rome admired in its popes.35 In both places, as
throughout Latin Mediterranean Europe, the image of the powerful but
caring *pius pater* was held up for bishops to imitate. The Book of the Popes,
or *Liber Pontificalis*, reserves special praise for those seventh-century popes
who promote church-building and who grant funerary bequests to the Roman
clergy.36 In their building activity the Roman bishops displayed fatherly
pietas not only to their flock, by providing them a house where they might
worship, but also to the fathers of the faith, that is, to the apostles, martyrs
and saints in whose honor and around whose relics these churches were
built.37 In their granting of funerary bequests, they displayed a special care,
a special *pietas*, for their clergy.

However much light this general sketch of Italian and Gallic episcopal
piety sheds on Wilfrid's behavior as bishop, it cannot substitute for a more
specialized investigation of particular bishops in Rome and Lyon during the
early seventh century. For it seems likely that a few recent examples of
episcopal leadership in each place--examples personally remembered by
people Wilfrid knew and respected--would have made a proportionately

---

35 Heinzelmann notes that there were also differences between what Gaul and Rome admired
in their respective bishops. In particular, the Gallic episcopal epitaphs make a point of
associating the bishop's virtues with his aristocratic birth and social standing. Although many
popes also had noble origins, little or nothing is made of that fact. The *Liber Pontificalis*, for
example, often mentions the geographical origin of a pope and sometimes his father and
mother, but it does not link the pope's origins--be they aristocratic or not--to his *virtutes*. For
Heinzelmann's discussion of the uniqueness of Gallic bishops in this regard, see pp. 237-238.

36 For building activity, see LP chs. 72, 75; for funerary bequests, see LP chs. 73, 74, and 77.

37 For more on the bishops' role in promoting the cults of the saints, see Brown, *The Cult of
the Saints* 8-9, 31-33.

greater impression on him than the many past ones could have. Just as some of these bishops showed him how a bishop must endure persecution, so did others among them show him how to behave as a *pius pater.*

Fatherly *Pietas* among the Early Seventh-Century Popes

An examination of certain exemplary popes between Gregory the Great, who died in 604, and Vitalian, who was consecrated pope in 657, proves especially instructive. These include Honorius (625-638), who was pope at the time of Wilfrid's birth, John IV (640-642), Theodore (642-649), Martin (649-654) and Eugenius (654-657). Either Martin or Eugenius was pope when Wilfrid arrived in Rome sometime in the early 650s.

No discussion of these early seventh-century popes can begin without briefly asking the question of Pope Gregory the Great's influence upon them. Although medieval historians have rightly emphasized Gregory's central role in shaping the later medieval church and papacy, his long-range influence seems to have been much greater than his influence on the popes who immediately succeeded him in the early to mid-seventh century. Although Anglo-Saxon England venerated Gregory with special fervency throughout the seventh and eighth centuries, Rome during the same period hardly remembered him at all. Peter Llewellyn has argued that the seventh-century Roman clergy came to regard monastic popes like Gregory and his disciple Honorius in a dim light. Good monks though they may have been, they were nevertheless remembered, in Gregory's case, as a weak advocate for the privileges of the secular Roman clergy and, in Honorius' case, as a poor defender against imperial attempts to compromise Rome's orthodoxy and deny her apostolic primacy (Llewellyn 363-365, 376). Honorius' capitulation to the Eastern doctrine of Monotheletism in 634 eventually proved so great an embarrassment to the Roman church that Pope Leo II fell in step with the Council of Constantinople and anathematized him in 682 for trying "with profane treachery to subvert the immaculate faith."[38]

Despite the shortcomings that the Roman clergy saw in these two popes, the Anglo-Saxon Wilfrid still would have found much in them,

---

38 Mansi 11:732, quoted in Richards 182.

especially Honorius, to emulate. Fond memories of both pontiffs doubtless lingered at the church in Canterbury, where Wilfrid spent a full year just before leaving for the continent in about 651 (LW ch. 3). Gregory the Great was especially revered at Canterbury and wherever else in England he planted Roman Christianity through Augustine's mission in 597. If Llewellyn is correct, however, the assessment of Gregory and the Gregorian tradition that Wilfrid probably heard in Rome must have differed sharply from what he had learned at home. Considering Wilfrid's lifelong concern to emulate the ways of the Roman church and clergy, one must conclude that however much Wilfrid continued to honor the memories of Gregory and Honorius, he must have had to revise his youthful assessment of them in light of what Roman clergy were saying about them in the early 650s.

Yet even a pope like Honorius, whom many perceived as so delinquent in protecting the orthodoxy of the Roman church, had many virtues that could yet be praised. With indomitable energy, for example, he built and repaired Rome's churches. In fact, the *Liber Pontificalis* reserves all praise of Honorius for this aspect of his papal ministry. Though an imitator of Gregory in most respects, in this one he departed radically from his mentor's example. Gregory did almost no church building during his pontificate, a fact which is probably due to Rome's then gloomy future. Between the pontificates of Gregory and Honorius, however, Rome's prospects grew brighter: schisms had been healed, the plague had abated, the Lombard menace had ceased, and pilgrims were flocking to Rome in ever increasing numbers. Responding to the flourishing pilgrim trade, Honorius instituted an ambitious program to transform old pagan buildings into churches, to refurbish Rome's old churches, and to build new ones. He changed the old Senate House, Senate Court, and the reception halls of grand mansions into the churches of St. Adrian, St. Lucia in Selcis, and the Quattro Coronati. In addition he replaced St. Peter's sixteen roof beams, recovered its roof with bronze removed from the temple of Venus, covered St. Peter's tomb and the church's main door with pure silver, and decorated various shrines within the church, also with silver. He also built from scratch, and decorated with equal munificence, the churches of St. Agnes, St. Pancras, St. Apollinaris, St. Cyriacus, and St. Severinus (LP ch. 72; Krautheimer 87).

Like Gregory, Honorius was a monk. He turned his mansion into a monastery and used monks, not secular clergy, on his staff.39 However difficult it is to reconcile Honorius' ascetic-monastic streak with his taste for newly built and lavishly decorated churches, both impulses dwelt within him. When Wilfrid first set foot in Rome, these new, magnificent churches and shrines surely brought Honorius to mind. He probably already knew of that pope as one who had taken special interest in evangelizing Wilfrid's native Northumbria and who, like Wilfrid himself, had been anxious to convert the Irish to the proper Easter observance (EH 2.17, 2.19). In this respect, at least, Honorius showed himself as one concerned to teach orthodoxy, his failure to reject Monothelitism notwithstanding.

The more closely one compares Wilfrid's episcopate with Honorius' pontificate, the more strikingly do parallels between the two emerge--so much so that one begins to suspect both that Wilfrid knew much about this pope, who had ruled during Wilfrid's infancy, and that Wilfrid saw him as worthy of imitation. Like Honorius, Wilfrid was a monk-bishop who devoted considerable energy and resources to church construction and maintenance. In good Honorian fashion, he repaired the roof and windows of the church at York, adorning it also with "various kinds of vessels and furniture"; he built the church at Ripon, decorating it with "gold and silver and varied purples"; and he built the Hexham church which, as Stephen reckons, was the grandest church north of the Alps (LW chs. 16, 17, 22). As a builder of churches, Wilfrid had no equal among the seventh-century bishops of Northumbria. Who then could have inspired Wilfrid to such activity? Although some have suggested the powerful bishops of Gaul, an equally likely candidate would be Honorius, whose churches and martyrs' shrines Wilfrid visited, perhaps daily, during his stay in Rome.40

---

39 Kelly 70. The inscription on Honorius' tomb shows that contemporaries saw him as a faithful imitator of Gregory the Great. It reads, in part, "Namque Gregorii tanti vestigia iusti / dum sequeris cupiens et meritumque geris" (De Rossi, *Inscriptiones* 127, qtd. in Duchesne 326, n. 19).

40 LW ch. 5. For the view that Gallic bishops exercised a decisive influence upon Wilfrid in this regard, see Mayr-Harting 132-134; see also Roper, "The Territorial Possessions" 170-177.

As admirable a *pius pater* as Honorius was, Wilfrid had good reason for not imitating him in every respect. As has already been shown, Honorius' defense of Roman orthodoxy was deemed to be grossly inadequate by the Roman church and clergy in the generation after his death. Between Wilfrid's birth (ca. 634) and his arrival in Rome some twenty years later, two easterners occupied the papal throne. They were John IV (640-642) from Dalmatia and Theodore (642-649) from Palestine.41 Many Greek-speaking ecclesiastics had come to Rome from the East in the mid-seventh century, disgruntled over growing imperial sympathy for heretics and schismatics.42 As members of this immigrant community, John and Theodore distinguished themselves by their tenacious defense of Roman orthodoxy. In their intolerance for heretics and schismatics, they proved more Roman than the Romans. With their minds well attuned to the subtleties of theological debate, they provided Rome with a strong line of defense against the Emperor's and patriarch's repeated assaults on orthodoxy. The native Roman clergy appreciated the help that easterners like Maximus, John IV, and Theodore I could give them. Such might succeed where native Italians like Honorius had failed.

The clergy's hopes were not disappointed. Soon after John IV was consecrated in 640, he moved quickly to convoke at Rome a synod that pronounced anathema upon Monothelete doctrine as the latter had been set forth in the imperial edict *Ekthesis* (Mansi 10:607, quoted in Richards 184). He then sent a letter to Emperor Constantine III, demanding that he tear down the copies of *Ekthesis* publicly displayed in Constantinople (Mansi 10:682f., quoted in Hefele 5:68). As concerned about heresy on the western front as on the eastern, John wrote a letter to certain bishops in Ireland exhorting them to root out "the poison of the Pelagian heresy" there. He also

---

41 They were only the first in a long line of thirteen Greek-speaking ecclesiastics who were elected to the papacy between 640 and 752. See Richards 270.

42 These eastern monks and clergy quickly became a powerful force in the Roman church. In 645 a group of monks from the convent of St. Sabbas in the Judean hills settled in Rome on the little Aventine; not long afterwards other oriental monasteries sprang up all over the city. For more on the emigration of Greek churchmen to Rome, see Krautheimer 90 and Bréhier 6-7.

expressed concern that certain among the Irish failed to observe the Catholic dating of Easter (EH 2.19).

Theodore, a native of Jerusalem, succeeded John as pope in 642. Typical of Rome's Greek-speaking clergy, Theodore worked hard to keep Roman orthodoxy pure and, like John, dared to incur the emperor's wrath in defense of that end.43 In addition, Theodore displayed a zeal for regulating church discipline and order strictly in accordance with established catholic canons. For example, when the emperor's disfavor drove Patriarch Pyrrhus from Constantinople in 641, Pope Theodore refused to acknowledge the newly appointed patriarch Paul as legitimate until Pyrrhus could be deposed canonically.44 Arguing from the apostle Paul's observation that a woman is bound to her husband until he was dead (Rom. 7.1-3), Theodore concluded that the Roman church was bound to Pyrrhus until Pyrrhus was "dead," either literally (*natura*) or canonically (*culpa*) (PL 87.78). In other words, Pyrrhus had to be tried, found guilty of a canonical offense, and excommunicated by a church synod before Paul could be recognized as patriarch.45

In the same way that Wilfrid would later echo Pope Honorius' concern for church building, so too did he echo Pope Theodore's concern for

---

43 In a letter to the newly crowned emperor, Constans, Theodore boldly demanded that *Ekthesis* be removed from the wall on which it was displayed and then burned. In that same letter he expressed amazement that the emperor had not yet issued a decree renouncing Monotheletism. This letter is extant only in Syriac and was translated into Latin by Cardinal Mai in *Novae Patrum bibliothecae* 6: 510-11. Jaffé included excerpts from it in the supplement to his 1875 edition of *Regesta Pontificum*, but ascribed it to Pope John IV, not Theodore. Later authors, however, have concluded that Mai was in fact correct in ascribing it to Pope Theodore. Mann did so explicitly (369); Richards implicitly (185). The information cited here concerning the content of Theodore's letter is taken from Jaffé's abridgment (2:739, s.v. "John IV").

44 In 641 Constans became emperor through a military coup. He then banished the empress Martina on suspicion of poisoning his father, Constantine III. Because Pyrrhus had been Martina's close ally, he fled Constantinople. Paul then assumed the patriarchate.

45 Pyrrhus had few admirers. The people of Constantinople reportedly hated him and rose up against him, while Theodore himself scorned him as a heretic. Theodore insisted, however, that even a heretical bishop cannot simply be hounded out of his office. He must be deposed canonically. As Theodore says in his letter to Paul, "For the rioting and the ill-will of the populace cannot deprive one of his episcopal rank" (PL 87.78). Much of this letter is translated in Hefele 5:70-71.

observing strictly Rome's sacred canons in all things, especially in matters having to do with episcopal succession. When, according to Stephen, Archbishop Theodore of Canterbury unlawfully consecrated three men as bishops over parts of Wilfrid's Northumbrian diocese, Wilfrid argued his case before a Roman synod along lines that recall Pope Theodore's claims against Paul. Just as Pope Theodore had argued that Pyrrhus could not be deprived of his patriarchate without being tried and found guilty of some *culpa*, so Wilfrid asserted that he had been robbed of his see without ever having been accused, much less tried and convicted, of any canonical *culpa* (ch. 30).

The popes of the mid-seventh century had good reason for caring so passionately about the observance of their church's canons. Devoid of any political or military might, the Roman church possessed those canons as the sole weapon to wield in its battle against both Monotheletism and the powerful alliance of emperor and patriarch that stood behind it. Some such weapon was badly needed to prevent the emperor from riding roughshod over the Roman church's jealously guarded privileges and its unspotted orthodoxy. Fueled by resentment over the Monothelite controversy, the imperial government subjected the Roman church between 638 and 656 to a veritable reign of terror: it exiled leaders of the Roman clergy and plundered the papal treasury for eight days in 638; it arrested and exiled the papal apocrisarius in Constantinople and destroyed his chapel at the Placidia Palace in 648-649; it arrested, condemned, and exiled Pope Martin, the abbot Maximus, and his disciple Anastasius between 653 and 655; and it announced plans to arrest and exile Pope Eugenius in 656.46

---

46 All these events are discussed in Richards 183-192. For the plundering in 638, see LP ch. 73; for the arrest and persecution of the apocrisarius and others and for the destruction of his chapel in 648-649, see LP ch. 76; for Pope Martin's ordeal, see LP ch. 76 (Martin), Martin, *Epp.* 14-17 in PL 87.197-204, and Anastasius, *Collectanea,* "Commemoratio eorum quae...acta sunt...in...Martinum papam" in PL 129.591-604; for Maximus' and Anastasius' arrest and trial, see Anastasius *Collectanea* "Relatio Motionis" in PL 129.603-624. The threat to Eugenius occurs in the following message from imperial agents to Abbot Maximus: "Verumtamen ut scias, domine abba, quoniam si saltem modicem requiem sumpserimus a confusione gentium, conjungi vobis habemus per sanctam Trinitatem, et papam qui nunc tollemus...et omnes vos conflabimus, unumquemque in apto sibi loco, ut conflatus est Martinus" (*Collectanea Anastasii Bibliocarii,* PL 129.654).

Such dangerous times demanded stalwart popes who could press their full knowledge of canon law into the service of restraining emperor and patriarch. The examples of these knowledgeable and intrepid churchmen could have hardly been lost on the pilgrim Wilfrid.47 Under their tutelage, Wilfrid learned "many rules of ecclesiastical discipline," including the rule for determining the date of Easter (LW ch. 5). If he had not sought to learn those rules before arriving in Rome, his first visit there would have inspired him to do so. The Roman church's situation in the early 650s would have made it clear to any casual observer that the church remains vulnerable to persecution, even in a nominally Christian empire. By appealing to the emperor's Christian identity as one bound to observe the canons of the church universal, the church of Rome possessed its most effective defense against imperial machinations. If any historical truth accrues to Stephen's picture of a Wilfrid who entrusts his defense to the ecclesiastical canons as they were preserved in Rome, then one can be sure that Wilfrid appropriated for himself the Roman church's insight about the value of knowing and scrupulously observing canon law.

Popes John IV, Theodore, and Martin were remembered by contemporaries primarily for their bravery in defending Rome's status as the arbiter of orthodoxy. By so doing, they exercised to the limit two of the bishop's most important fatherly duties: teaching and judging. In addition to these two duties, the *Liber Pontificalis* and seventh-century papal funerary inscriptions mention at least three other duties that seventh-century Romans liked their bishops to fulfill. One is generosity to the poor: Pope Boniface V (619-625) is said to have given out his own fortune in alms, and to have helped "phalanxes of orphans"48; Severinus (640) is praised as one who was "kind to all men, a lover of the poor, generous and most gentle"; and

---

47 Dorothy Whitelock notes that in comparison to Northumbria's Celtic-trained clergy, "Wilfrid was better placed to see the disadvantages of haphazard arrangements and lack of organization" ("Bede" 33). Although Whitelock does not ask why Wilfrid was "better placed to see" them, a look at the Rome Wilfrid would have known during his first pilgrimage there gives the beginnings of an answer.

48 DeRossi, *Inscriptiones* 128: "Nam vidualis apex pupillorumque falanges caecorumque chorus dux tibi lucis erit."

Theodore (642-649) is celebrated as "a lover of the poor, generous, kind and merciful to all." Another duty, as mentioned earlier, is the granting of funerary bequests to the clergy: Popes Deusdedit (615-618), Boniface V (619-625), John IV (640-642), Eugenius (654-657), Agatho (678-681), and Benedict (682-683) are all praised specifically for this virtue. Although Honorius outstripped all others in devotion to the building, repair, and decoration of Churches, other popes ranked it highly on their list of priorities. In this area perhaps more than any other, the *Liber Pontificalis* entries for this period take special pains to record who did what. Besides Honorius, Boniface IV (608-615), Boniface V (619-625), Severinus (640), John IV (640-642), and Theodore (642-649) are all cited for building new churches or restoring old ones.

As with the other celebrated episcopal virtues, Stephen ascribes these three to Wilfrid. He cites Wilfrid's generosity to the laity at least four times, noting especially the alms which he gave to the poor, the orphan, the widow, and the sick (LW chs. 8, 11, 21 and 62(63)). He also states that Wilfrid gave gifts to his clergy with unequaled munificence, and reports how Wilfrid, shortly before his death, divided his treasury into four parts, allotting one part of it to his loyal clergy, another part to the poor, and another to the churches of St. Mary and St. Paul in Rome (LW chs. 21 and 62(63)). Finally, Stephen celebrates Wilfrid's church construction activities in a way which imitates the *Liber Pontificalis* (LW chs. 16, 17 and 22). In every respect, those fatherly virtues which seventh-century Rome admired in her popes, Stephen ascribes to Wilfrid.

Fatherly *Pietas* among the Archbishops of Lyon

Much of what Wilfrid observed of Rome's episcopal traditions, he would have also seen in Lyon. Unfortunately, history has left a much scanter record of Lyon's seventh-century bishops than it has of Rome's. Nevertheless, as the occupant of Gaul's most ancient see, Lyon's archbishop enjoyed a primacy of honor surpassed by no other bishop in Merovingian Gaul. Early medieval Lyon celebrated many of the same fatherly virtues in her bishops as Rome did in hers. Sidonius Apollinaris praises Lyon's bishop

Patiens (ca. 480) for building new churches, repairing old ones, and feeding the poor (*Ep.* 6.12, pp. 101-102); and the great Nicetius (ca. 575) is revered time and time again for his generosity to the needy and his love for the people and clergy of Lyon.49

Wilfrid's alleged mentor, Archbishop Annemundus, appears as one cast in the same mold. The anonymous author of his eighth-century *Acta* reports that he was Gallo-Roman by nationality, that his father and brother were both *praefecti*, and that he had been raised in the *praetorium* of Kings Dagobert I and Clovis II. Having lived his whole life among aristocracy and royalty, he moved easily amid men of power and was fully counted as one of them. In every aspect of his work and life as bishop, Annemundus embodied the late Antique Gallic episcopal ideal. Like Nicetius before him, he may have been hand-picked for the Lyon episcopate by his predecessor Viventius (AsA chs. 2-3).

The author of the *Acta* relates almost nothing about the specifically churchly activities of Annemundus' episcopate. He emphasizes instead Annemundus' martyrdom, which has already been discussed, and his pastoral activities as provider and protector. Among these activities, one bears special mention since Stephen mentions it in connection with Wilfrid, but the *Liber Pontificalis* does not report it as an activity characteristic of seventh-century popes. That activity is to assume the role of godfather and advisor to young kings. As his *Acta* reports, Archbishop Annemundus adopted the boy king Clotar III as his godson and counselled him in secular matters as well as ecclesiastical. His close relations with the young king made him both a man of power and an object of envy. So great was his influence over Clotar that other kings and nobles granted him whatever he sought. Yet, however kindly the bishop may have appeared to Wilfrid or other young disciples whom he may have taken under his wing, certain members of the royal assembly

---

49 In Gregory of Tours' *Liber vitae patrum*, Nicetius' predecessor in the see of Lyon extols the young Nicetius as "amator castimoniae dilectorque ecclesiarum et in elymosinis valde devotus" (8.3, 693). Similarly, Nicetius is praised in his epitaph with the words: "vir bonus, indultus cunctis famulisque benignus /...verbere quisque suo, mansuetus patiens mitis venerabilis aptus, / pauperibus promptus simplicibusque pius" (Diehl 209, no. 1073.7-10).

mistrusted him and accused him of secretly trying to ruin Clotar's reign (AsA ch. 2).

The author of Annemundus' *Acta* takes pains to show that the archbishop's immense secular power neither corrupted him nor kept him from executing the duties of his office with justice, kindness and compassion. The narrative of his *passio* relates how, before his martyrdom, he implored his clergy and the populace to remember him kindly, saying, "I beseech you, my brethren and all the people, and humbly beg that, if I have appeared unpleasant to you in any way or taken away anything violently, that you not think ill of me, but forgive me peaceably." His flock, however, could not bear their doomed bishop's self-reproach and responded with one voice, "Never, good Pastor, have you been unpleasant to us, nor have you ever taken anything from us by force; on the contrary, all of us from the least to the greatest, consider ourselves to have been enriched and comforted by your kindnesses" (AsA chs. 5-6; cf. 1 Sam. 12.4). Like the epitaphs on the tombs of fifth- and sixth-century Gallic bishops, the eighth-century author of Annemundus' *Acta* remembers his martyred hero as one whose immense power did not diminish his fatherly *pietas*. He provided for and protected every member of his flock, "from the least to the greatest."

Wilfrid's Hybrid Episcopal Piety

In his important chapter on Wilfrid, Mayr-Harting distinguishes between the Gallic and the Roman influences upon the development of Wilfrid's episcopal piety. On the one hand, he associates Wilfrid's worldly episcopal might with the examples of powerful Gallic bishops like Annemundus; on the other he associates Wilfrid's mild missionary methods with the example of Rome, and most especially, Gregory the Great (132-137, 145-147). As this chapter has shown, such a distinction may be too facile. For one thing, what was Roman for Wilfrid was not necessarily Gregorian. The Rome that he saw in the 650s and the style of episcopal leadership that he witnessed there probably owed little to Gregory's influence and may even have been reacting against it. For another, the popes of the mid-seventh century showed themselves every bit as capable as their Gallic counterparts of wielding immense authority, standing up to secular power, building magnificent churches, and patronizing their flock. Certain local variations in practice and piety must never obscure the common Latin Mediterranean heritage that the churches in Rome and Gaul shared. Within that heritage there emerged an ideal of episcopal leadership which, in its broadest outlines, men like Cyprian, Ambrose, Augustine, Gelasius, Nicetius of Lyon, Annemundus, Honorius, and Martin embraced.

However little Wilfrid's actual behavior as bishop may have resembled that of these great episcopal exemplars, his episcopal ideal in its broadest outlines seems to have approximated theirs better than it did the more purely ascetic ideal of Martin of Tours, Columba, or Cuthbert. If Stephen faithfully reproduced the former ideal in his *Life*, it becomes clear that Wilfrid's ideal bishop was a hybrid of two Christ-types, that of the persecuted apostle-martyr and the *pius pater*. With respect to both types in this hybrid, he learned much from noting the concrete behaviors of particular bishops whom he came to know or learn about during his first pilgrimage-- men like Popes Honorius, Theodore and Martin and Archbishop Annemundus of Lyon. From the episcopal martyrs Martin and Annemundus, he learned that bishops in the seventh century, no less than those in the pre-Constantinian age, must suffer persecution from men generally and from secular rulers particularly. Having learned that lesson, he was prepared, as bishop, to endure continual persecution at the hands of Northumbria's Kings Ecgfrith and Aldfrith for more than twenty-five years.

From each of such fatherly types as Honorius, John IV, Theodore, Martin, and Annemundus, he learned a different aspect of what would become central to his own fatherly persona. From Honorius, he learned how to be simultaneously a Benedictine-styled monk and a powerful bishop who could build and decorate churches lavishly and exhort kings to keep and propagate the faith. From Annemundus' relations with the boy-king Clotar, he learned how to function as father and counsellor to kings, as he did to Caedwalla of Wessex and Osred of Northumbria. From Popes John IV, Theodore and Martin, and from the strong tradition of canon law in Lyon, he learned that it is incumbent upon God's bishops to revere and enforce canon

law even when so doing may bring persecution from secular authorities.50
From Popes Severinus, John IV, and Eugenius, he learned that a generous
funerary bequest might demonstrate his gratitude and generosity to the
clergy who had remained fiercely loyal to him during times of trial.51 And
finally, from the likes of Lyon's archbishops Patiens, Nicetius and
Annemundus, as well as from popes John IV, Theodore, and Eugenius, he
learned a fatherly generosity that benefitted the poor, the orphan, and the
stranger.

In chapter 36 of the *Life of Wilfrid*, Stephen depicts Wilfrid
encouraging his comrades to remain firm in the faith, despite the persecution
they are suffering with him. Reminding them of the examples of the
patriarchs, prophets, Christ, and the apostles, Wilfrid cites for them a verse
from Hebrews, saying: "And so, my brothers and helpers in Christ, since we,
according to the excellent teacher, have so great a cloud of witnesses in our
midst, let us run with patience the race before us." Whereas chapters two
and three of this book tried to show how Stephen uses this scriptural "cloud
of witnesses" to portray Wilfrid as persecuted confessor and devoted father,
the present chapter has attempted to show how another cloud of witnesses,
namely, certain bishops of early seventh-century Rome and Lyon, may have
inspired Bishop Wilfrid to believe and behave as he did. Stephen mentions
nothing about any of these bishops, except Annemundus. Yet during his first
pilgrimage to Rome, Wilfrid must have been made aware both of their
existence and, more importantly, of their greatness. If he had not observed
such greatness for himself, the pious citizens of Rome and Lyon, men like
Rome's archdeacon Boniface, could hardly have failed to point it out to him
(LW ch. 5). As a young and impressionable pilgrim, one can imagine the
earnestness with which Wilfrid would have heard them out. Such stories as

---

50 Hubert Mordek has argued that the *Collectio Vetus Gallica*, the earliest systematic
collection of canon law in the medieval Latin West, was compiled in Lyon in about 600 (78-79).
According to E. A. Lowe, early medieval Lyon had several flourishing, episcopally controlled
scriptoria (8) that produced, among other things, an abundance of canon legal documents. At
least two such manuscripts are extant (Lowe 17; Coville 507).

51 The *Liber Pontificalis* describes such bequests as *integra roga*. See Richards 263-265; LP
chs. 73, 74, and 77.

were told about each city's episcopal heroes--and such dramas involving martyred bishops as Wilfrid observed for himself--probably meant less to Wilfrid as history (or external history) than as sacred (or internal) history. These contemporary bishops were doubtless presented to him as virtuous men not in their own right, but because they faithfully incarnated the heroic Christ-types of Scripture in their own persons. As such, their lives and deaths were interepreted through the lens of Scripture. What is often forgotten, however, is that in good dialectical fashion, Scripture was interpreted in turn for the likes of Wilfrid through the lens of these bishops' lives and deaths. In other words, the scriptural stories about the prophets, the apostles and, above all, Christ acquired meaning for Wilfrid through experiencing concretely these bishops' lives and passions for himself and through hearing stories that faithful, remembering admirers told about them.

In the same way that Wilfrid encouraged his comrades to imitate prophets and apostles, so would he have sought to imitate them himself as he had seen them already imitated in the bishop-martyrs and bishop-fathers of Rome and Lyon. Yet to imitate Christ in this way carries with it a system of deep, existential convictions about the nature of human life, about God's activity within it, and about how one should properly respond to that divine activity. That system of convictions, though Christian, nevertheless came into conflict with another system, equally Christian. This latter system grew out of a more rigorously ascetic Anglo-Celtic tradition that held up Cuthbert and Aidan, not Wilfrid or Annemundus, as the highest episcopal exemplars. By comparing the two episcopal ideals as each tradition presents it, the final chapter will attempt to articulate the deep convictions behind each one and, by so doing, will show once and for all that the rivalry between Wilfrid's disciples and Cuthbert's, and more fundamentally, between the so-called Roman and Celtic factions, was motivated not just by petty partisan rivalries, but by a deep and abiding theological difference.

CHAPTER FIVE

THE DEBATE OVER SANCTITY--
REMEMBERING WILFRID AND CUTHBERT

So far this study has identified two main images which dominate Stephen's depiction of Wilfrid. The first is Wilfrid as persecuted man of God. By means of this image, Stephen shows his hero to be the fulfillment of the types of prophet, apostle, and martyr. The second image is Wilfrid as *pius pater* who, in the roles of bishop and abbot, shows fatherly concern for the laity, his secular priests, his monastic *familia*, and his various royal protégés. In the previous chapter, we explored the possibility that these two images which Stephen presents grew out of Wilfrid's own understanding of his life and mission as that understanding had been shaped in his youth, especially during his first pilgrimage to Rome in the mid-650s. Again and again we have noted how apparently unique was Wilfrid's understanding of apostolic discipleship and fatherly stewardship among Northumbrian bishops of the seventh and early eighth centuries. Unlike such figures as Aidan, Chad, Cuthbert and John of Beverley, whose understandings of self and mission derived in large part from the Christian spirituality of Iona, Wilfrid appears to have drawn much more from the Latin Christian spirituality of late antique Rome and Lyon.

This chapter will explore the theological significance of the convictions that shaped the piety of Wilfrid and his *familia* and will attempt to assess the special message that those convictions conveyed to early Christian Northumbria, a culture whose religious core had been largely

108

forged in an Irish monastic tradition mediated through Iona. Associated with each brand of spirituality, the Latin (or Roman) and the Ionan, are two different convictions about the evils which most readily threaten human life and about how God redeems human life from them. Associated with each set of convictions, in turn, are different understandings of human sanctity. As the first chapter noted, the early medieval imagination, following Augustine's lead, recognized a particular person as saint precisely because he or she was seen to point beyond himself or herself to the reality of God. Distinct modes or styles of sanctity signified, each in its own way, different understandings of God, different theologies. Although those differences may have had more to do with emphasis than substance, they could be highly charged with emotional as well as theological significance.

Each mode of sanctity testified in its own way and from its own peculiar perspective to how God has intervened, and continues to intervene, in human life. Taken together, such different understandings may have complemented each other and served to remind the faithful of the myriad and surprising ways in which redemption occurs. On the other hand, if one mode of sanctity tried to establish itself as normative and did so in such a way that other modes were excluded, then the community that recognized this mode as normative laid itself open to the charge of idolatry. For by attaching all its admiration to this particular mode of sanctity, it may have come to identify a particular evil, which its favorite saint encounters, with evil in general; or a particular saving act of God, with God's salvation in general. The danger of such identification lay in its refusal to recognize other forms of evil and in its tendency to deny the testimony of those who have honestly experienced those other forms as the source of life's most acute suffering. This issue will be addressed in greater detail at the chapter's end.

A careful comparison of the anonymous Lindisfarne monk's *Life of Cuthbert* and Stephen's *Life of Bishop Wilfrid*, two saints' Lives which express very different traditions of spirituality, will reveal that neither text is eager to acknowledge the particular evil and good to which the other text testifies. This fact becomes all the more curious when one considers that their respective subjects, the historical Cuthbert and Wilfrid, had so much in common.

Despite the striking similarities between them, these two men are depicted as moving in different spiritual worlds. We have no record that they ever met each other. Cuthbert's name never appears in Stephen's *Life*, although Stephen twice copies verbatim from the *Anonymous Life of Cuthbert*, nor does Wilfrid's name ever appear either in the anonymous' *Life* or in Bede's *Prose Life*.1 And yet each man moved in the same royal and ecclesiastical circles and even had common friends. In both *Lives* one encounters the abbesses Aebbe and Aelfflaed, Kings Ecgfrith and Aldfrith, Queen Iurminburg, and others.2

Besides this mutual silence, certain signs indicate a history of tension between these men and their worlds. For example, in about 660 King Alhfrith drove Cuthbert and his monastic brethren, led by Abbot Eata, away from their monastery at Ripon in order to install a new monastic community there with Wilfrid as its abbot (LCP ch. 8). According to Bede, Alhfrith, having been enlightened by Wilfrid, had grown impatient with the original community's Irish ways (EH 3.25).

In another place Bede relates that during the year after Cuthbert's death, the Lindisfarne church underwent such great trials that many of its brethren decided to leave. Peace returned the next year when Eadberht became bishop (LCP ch. 40). Although Bede never identifies explicitly the cause of these trials, he casually mentions in another place that Wilfrid ruled over Lindisfarne during the year between Cuthbert's death and Eadberht's accession (687-688) (EH 4.29). Colgrave has suggested that Wilfrid caused the trouble for the Lindisfarne community, either by trying to impose a pure Benedictine observance upon it or by trying to usurp the traditionally pre-eminent authority that Lindisfarne's abbot had always exercised over the

---

1 For the places where Stephen copies from the LCA, compare LW Praefatio and LCA Praefatio; LW ch. 11 and LCA 4.1.

2 Aebbe: LW chs. 37 and 39; LCA 2.3; cf. LCP ch. 10. Aelfflaed: LW ch. 60; LCA 3.6, 4.10; cf. LCP chs. 23, 24, 34. King Ecgfrith: LW chs. 17, 19-20, 24, 33 et al.; LCA 3.6, 4.7, 4.8; cf. LCP chs. 24, 27. King Aldfrith: LW chs. 43-47, 58-59; LCA 3.6, 4.3; cf. LCP ch. 24. Queen Iurminburg: LW ch. 24; LCA 4.8. Bede's *Prose Life* even mentions a Lindisfarne abbot named Cudda (LCP ch. 37), who may have been the monk to whom Wilfrid ministered there (LW ch. 2).

entire community, including the bishop (*Two Lives* 357). Beneath the mutual
silence, and the scarcely mentioned lordship that Wilfrid exercised over
Lindisfarne after Cuthbert's death, a quiet conflict probably had been
brewing between these two men for quite some time. That conflict mirrored
their different experiences of (and convictions about) how the power of God
works to redeem human life. That conflict, however, was not theirs alone. It
had been fought in one form or another ever since the meeting of the Roman
and Ionan missions on Northumbrian soil and had been settled technically,
but only technically, at the Synod of Whitby in 664. For behind Whitby's
debates about the dating of Easter and the shape of the tonsure lay a deeper
debate about the legitimacy of these two different traditions, each of which
viewed the nature of God, the world, evil, the church, and human sanctity in
its own distinct way.3

Two Types of Christlike Discipleship: Asceticism and Martyrdom

This study has as its special concern the form of human sanctity that
each tradition held up as worthy of imitation. For both, sanctity implied
imitating Christ and such Christ-types as the prophet, apostle, and martyr.
Yet within each tradition, imitating Christ and his types had a peculiar
meaning, a meaning that was largely bound up with a particular
understanding of the kind of sacrifice that a true imitator of Christ must
make.

An example will illustrate the point. Both the anonymous Lindisfarne
monk and Stephen designate Cuthbert and Wilfrid, respectively, as *confessor.*
Each author, however, understands the *confessor* designation differently (cf.
Appendix IV). The Lindisfarne monk uses it quite generally to mean anyone
who bears witness to the truth of Christ's life and preaching. He uses the
word *martyr* in exactly this same general sense. Both terms connote a

---

3 In the sacramental world of the early Middle Ages, where everything signifies a greater
reality, issues like the shape of the tonsure and the dating of Easter can assume a significance
which seems ludicrous to the modern observer. In much the same way that I have approached
the ritual of pilgrimage in chapter 4, Edward James has appealed to the insights of cultural
anthropology to help explain what was at stake in the tonsure question (93-94).

Christlike suffering that may take almost any form, including such voluntary forms as bodily renunciation and pilgrimage. By contrast, Stephen uses both terms in their much more primitive and restricted sense. To be a martyr for him is to suffer persecution and death because of one's Christlike witness to the power of God; to be a confessor is to suffer persecution or life-threatening danger for the same reason, but not to the point of death. The essential and common element in both terms is a persecution instigated by others. Dalfinus thus merits being called a martyr because he suffered persecution and death at the hand of Queen Balthild; but Wilfrid, though eager for the "prize of martyrdom," merits only the title "confessor" since he suffered life-threatening danger from Dalfinus' persecutors, but did not actually die.4 Since Cuthbert did not suffer persecution at all, Stephen would not designate him by either term. The anonymous monk, on the other hand, designates him by both.5

Corresponding to these different understandings of what it means to be a confessor are similar divergences on what it means to have apostolic and prophetic qualities (cf. Appendix IV). It has already been shown that for Stephen, and perhaps for Wilfrid, those qualities include above all the patient endurance of persecution. Just as the prophet Elijah was persecuted by Queen Jezebel, the apostle Peter by Herod, and the apostle Andrew by the proconsul Aegeas, so too does Stephen see Wilfrid as having been persecuted by Kings Ecgfrith, Aldfrith, and others. When he announces at the end of the *Life* that Wilfrid has been made equal to the apostles Peter and Andrew, he simply means that like these apostles, Wilfrid patiently suffered persecution while faithfully executing his divine calling and that as a result God glorified him. Although the anonymous Lindisfarne monk asserts that Cuthbert also displays apostolic and prophetic qualities, their distinguishing mark has nothing to do with suffering persecution. It has rather to do with Cuthbert's spiritual powers, especially his ability to heal the sick and to foretell the future. As bishop, Cuthbert is thus described as one

4 Stephen calls Wilfrid a confessor again when Ecgfrith persecutes him by imprisoning him in Dunbar (ch. 38).

5 *Martyr*: LCA 4.15, 16, 17; *confessor*: LCA 4.16, 18.

who has "apostolic foresight" and who, like the apostles, worked many "signs and wonders," almost all of which were wonders of healing.6 These powers function as signs of Cuthbert's divine election and point back to other qualities which illuminate his radical faithfulness. In large measure, those qualities are those of the monk-ascetic, and include frequent prayer, the keeping of vigils, the gracious reception of guests, fasting, mortification of the flesh, avoidance of worldly honors, and poverty of dress.7 Cuthbert is thus shown to be an ascetic in the tradition of St. Antony and, more especially, St. Martin of Tours.

How should one understand theologically this ascetic type of sanctity? How does it see Christ as its type? Recalling Paul's understanding of the typical Christlike experience, the reader of the *Anonymous Life* can discern the basic dialectic to which Cuthbert's experience conforms. On the one hand, through humility and ascetic self-renunciation Cuthbert continually experiences death-like or hopeless situations which threaten to render God's promise of blessing untrustworthy. On the other, through the radical trusting of faith Cuthbert also experiences God's miraculous and redemptive intervention to bring about blessing where doom seems sure. In chapter two, we discussed how that same fundamental dialectic was at work in Stephen's portrayal of Wilfrid's experiences. What distinguishes Cuthbert's Christlike experience from Wilfrid's, however, is the manner in which he experiences the death-like situation, the manner in which he and others experience evil.

When evil strikes in the world of the Cuthbert *Life*, it almost always does so at a biological or organismic level. Attacking demons appear in the form of a disease which threatens the life of the bodily organism. Hopeless situations take the form of bodily want: a lack of food, warmth, or shelter--a lack which underscores the human being's radical organismic vulnerability and dependence upon nature. For the anonymous monk of Lindisfarne, estrangement from the natural world looms large in his mind as the tragic consequence of Adam's Fall. He is acutely aware of the struggle in which

6 LCA 4.10--"apostolicam providentiam"; LCA 4.2--"in signis et prodigiis."

7 Frequent prayer and vigils--1.5, 1.6, 2.1, 2.3, 3.3, 4.9; reception of guests--2.2; fasting--2.1; mortification of the flesh--2.3; avoidance of worldly honors and poverty of dress--4.1.

humanity and nature are engaged. He knows that bodily agony need not have plagued childbirth, that the ground upon which human beings walk was not always cursed, and that men and women did not always have to sweat and toil to wrest from nature life's necessities (Gen. 3.16-19).

Yet the anonymous author sees nature as the place where human beings encounter not only evil, but their redemption from it. God's miraculous intervention in history restores right relationship with nature. Such right relationship with nature, however, points beyond itself to the more fundamental right relationship with God, a relationship characterized by radical Christ-like faith. Cuthbert is presented as the paradigm of such faith. Twice he journeys forth without making provisions for food, trusting God to provide (LCA 2.4-5). In the same way, his ascetic life requires radical faith. As guest-master at Ripon, he is required by the monastic rule of hospitality to give the bread so necessary for his own and his community's life to the wayfaring stranger. Such an act signifies the monk's faith that the stranger who consumes the bread necessary for the monk's own organismic existence does not impoverish his life, but enriches it, as if the stranger were Christ or an angel (LCA 2.2). Cuthbert's fasting, which deprives the body of food, and his bathing in the North Sea, which deprives the body of warmth, require like faith (LCA 2.1, 2.3).

Precisely because he exposes himself again and again to the worst that nature has to offer--and deprives himself of its best--Cuthbert shatters the demonic conviction about nature which enslaves human life, namely, that the death-dealing powers which men and women experience in nature--disease, hunger, famine, and exposure--have ultimate control over human life. Hence, whereas others show great alarm at the sight of a house ablaze, Cuthbert correctly sees the fire as an illusion of the devil (LCA 2.6). The fire is demonic for two reasons: first, because it reinforces his audience's false conviction that one's house is one's ultimate shelter from the natural elements, and second, because it interferes with Cuthbert's teaching and baptizing, two activities which aim at liberating his hearers from their false convictions.8 By contrast, Cuthbert is established in right relationship with

---

8 A story that conveys the same fundamental message is found in LCA 2.7.

114

God and with nature through his radical faith. Much like Adam before the Fall, he enjoys communion with and dominion over nature: an eagle brings him food (2.5), sea animals warm his feet with their breath (2.3), the sea brings him wood (3.4), and ravens seek his forgiveness (3.5).9

Stephen's *Life of Bishop Wilfrid* knows almost nothing of this attitude which sees nature as that place where human beings experience evil and good, death and life, alienation and redemption most acutely. The social rather than the organismic aspect of human life preoccupies Stephen. When evil strikes, it destroys the delicate matrix of human community which is held so tenuously together by bonds of goodwill. If evil takes the form of bodily death, it severs family and filial bonds--relations between mother and son, father and son, bishop and *familia*.10 If it takes the more dangerous form of jealousy or envy--sins which Stephen ascribes specifically to Satanic activity-- it pits king against bishop, bishop against bishop, tradition against tradition, and priests against priests.11 From this perspective, estrangement among persons rather than estrangement from nature emerges as the Fall's most disturbing sign of lost communion with God. Just as fractured relations arose between Adam and Eve, Cain and Abel, so will all future human relationships replicate those of the primal family.

In the *Life of Bishop Wilfrid*, persons of high temporal status bear the marks of human fallenness most dramatically. When Wilfrid and others of God's elect suffer, they do so at the hands of wicked queens, persecuting kings, dukes and reeves of evil intent, and Satan-possessed archbishops.12

---

9 Parallel accounts occur, respectively, in LCP chs. 12, 10, 21, and 20.

10 LW chs. 2, 6, and 64(65)-65(66).

11 King against bishop--e.g., LW chs. 24, 45; bishop against bishop (Wilfrid vs. Theodore)-- LW ch. 24; and tradition vs. tradition (Rome vs. Iona)--LW ch. 10; Wilfrid's priests against others--LW ch. 49.

12 Besides Kings Ecgfrith and Aldfrith, temporal authorities who attack Wilfrid or Wilfrid's friends include: the Frankish queen Balthild and her dukes (LW ch. 6), Northumbria's King Oswiu (ch. 14), the Frankish duke Ebroin (ch. 27), Northumbria's Queen Iurminburg (ch. 24), Mercia's King Aethilred and his queen (ch. 40) and West Saxon King Centwini and his queen (ch. 40). Ecclesiastical persecutors include Archbishop Theodore of Canterbury (ch. 24),

The refusal of these latter to submit to God's authority as mediated successively through Christ, Peter, the church of Rome, and Wilfrid becomes a type for Adam's disobedience. Yet just as nature is portrayed in the Cuthbert *Life* as the place of both suffering and redemption, so do kings and other temporal lords display a double aspect in the Wilfrid *Life*. They are either "wolves" or "lambs," and their status as one or the other depends on their willingness to submit in faith to God's sovereign authority as it is made known to them through the teaching, customs, and discipline of the Roman church (LW ch. 24). Types of the good, obedient king--like Alhfrith and Caedwalla--adopt Roman ways in accordance with Wilfrid's counsel; types of the disobedient king maltreat him. Few, however, embody absolutely either type. Mercia's King Aethilred, Northumbria's Queen Iurminburg, and even Archbishop Theodore of Canterbury all appear first as wicked, then as saintly, depending upon whether they treat Wilfrid ill or well. In addition, royal fortunes stand or fall on the king's relations with Wilfrid. As Stephen relates concerning Ecgfrith's reign,

> When King Ecgfrith lived in concord with our bishop, he increased his kingdom through triumphant victories--as many will testify. But when that concord between them grew languid . . . the triumph of the King ended. (LW ch. 24)

Whereas the *Life of St. Cuthbert* expresses reconciliation with God in terms of reconciliation with nature, the *Life of Bishop Wilfrid* expresses it in terms of reconciliation with one's fellows. As one author has recently noted, the ideal of peace permeates Stephen's narrative (Isenberg 81-88). It is the *telos* toward which the entire work moves, especially after chapter 24. Peace characterized Adam's relationship with Eve before the Fall; peace will characterize relations between the saints in paradise. In the meantime, fallen humanity knows only dimly that human concord and solidarity.

For Stephen and Wilfrid, the orthodox and universal Roman church was the crucial sign of that solidarity. By strictly adhering to its customs, Wilfrid offered a critique to the Ionan churches which, by continuing in their own local, singular tradition, denied the call to universal brotherhood that the mid-seventh-century Roman church had come to represent not only for

---

various greedy bishops and abbots (ch. 46), nameless churchmen who excommunicated Wilfrid's followers (ch. 49) and a nameless Frankish bishop (ch. 33).

the Anglo-Saxon Wilfrid, but for "almost the whole world."13 Even the southern Irish had fallen under the powerful spell of unity and charity that Rome symbolized. The Irish abbot Cummian reports that when a delegation of the southern Irish visited Rome in the second quarter of the seventh century to observe Easter practices there, its members became eager for Ireland to abandon its time-honored traditions and to observe what they saw in Rome to be worldwide custom. He relates the experience of the Irish delegates as follows:

> They stayed in a hospice in the church of St. Peter together with a Greek, Palestinian, Scythian and Egyptian at Easter (of which our celebration differed from theirs by a whole month); and they swore to us before relics, saying: "Throughout the entire world, this dating of Easter is celebrated." And we declare that the power of God is contained in the relics of the holy martyrs and in the writings which they have brought back [to Ireland]. For we have seen with our own eyes a girl totally blind open her eyes, a paralytic walk, and many demons exorcised through these relics. (PL 87.977B-978A)

Such was the power of Rome's relics. In them was harnessed a divine power which made human life whole, in both its natural and social dimensions. Like the pilgrims of which Cummian speaks, Wilfrid too must have been struck by the uniformity of thought, feeling and ritual practice amongst the ethnically, regionally and linguistically diverse pilgrims in Rome. Here he would have seen, as did the Irish delegation before him, that Rome's custom was not merely one among many, but the one that reflected the orthodox custom of almost all the world, except Northumbria, parts of Scotland, and northern Ireland.

If the members of Cummian's Irish delegation brought home the power of Rome in its relics, Wilfrid did so in its customs, norms, discipline and laws. For Wilfrid all these things constituted "God's law," which any good bishop should teach. The Roman Church's special status as teacher of God's law did not derive from any special supernatural knowledge that it had. It had no unique or original claim to most of the canons and customs which it taught. It did have, however, a reputation for participating in and abiding by the ecumenical councils that had authoritatively adopted those

---

13 LW ch. 10: "Haec ratio disciplinae apostolicae sedis est et paene totius mundi...."

canons. Rome's authority as a teaching church thus derived from the fact that it faithfully followed and obeyed what the worldwide church had decreed in its councils rather than from what it had uniquely promulgated itself. Since Rome honored Christ by honoring the decrees of the councils, Christ through the councils returned the honor by conferring upon Rome a special authority. In the words of Maximus the Confessor,

> He speaks in vain who...does not satisfy and implore the most blessed papa of the most holy church of the Romans, that is, the Apostolic See which has received universal and supreme dominion, authority, and power of binding and loosing over all the holy churches of God throughout the world, from the incarnate Son of God Himself and also by all holy councils. (PL 129.576)

Through the apostolic see of Rome, God in Christ has imposed an order upon the entire church, calling all churches of the world to a single, harmonious, apostolic communion. Unlike the later sixteenth-century Protestant Reformers, men like Maximus the Confessor and Wilfrid experienced that order not as tyrannical, but as redemptive, as a type of the order that God imposed on the entire creation at the beginning of the world. Through divine law, which prescribes the nature of that order, God's worldwide church is rescued from the social chaos and anarchy that self-willed kings, emperors, schismatics, and heresiarchs bring against it. For Stephen, as probably for Wilfrid, that law was manifest in Scripture as well as in the creedal, liturgical, and canonical norms observed in the apostolic church of Rome. Moreover, it was through that law that God was seen as having dealings with God's elect. Just as God had related to Israel through Torah as interpreted through the prophets, so does God relate to the church through a new revelation of Law as taught by Jesus, handed down through Peter and the apostles, and authoritatively interpreted by the apostolic see of Rome. For Stephen, to live within that Church meant to observe fully its law as Wilfrid did, every "jot and tittle" of it (LW ch. 57; cf. Mt. 5.18).

The two visions of Fall and Redemption which the Cuthbert and Wilfrid *Lives* separately represent do not exclude each other. Although Stephen mentions persecution most consistently in connection with apostolicity and sanctity, he also extols radical asceticism in Wilfrid and in a Cuthbert-like hermit of the Ripon *familia* named Caelin, whom Stephen depicts as having Wilfrid's deepest admiration (LW chs. 21 and 63(64)). Nevertheless, the evils associated with the ascetic type do not loom large in Stephen's narrative. The concern for bodily disease, exposure, and famine hardly appears at all there. The animals never befriend Wilfrid as they do Cuthbert. By the same token, the evils associated with the type of the persecuted martyr never figure prominently in the anonymous' Cuthbert *Life*. The problem of Cuthbert's relationship with secular authority--the problem which figures most prominently in Wilfrid's *Life*--never really arises. Indeed, not a Northumbrian King or royal woman is mentioned who does not revere the holy man. Like the *Anonymous Life*, Bede's *Prose Life of Cuthbert* also gives a rosy picture of Cuthbert's relations with Northumbrian royalty. King Ecgfrith wants Cuthbert to be bishop so badly that he sails to Cuthbert's hermitage on Farne Island, falls at the saint's feet, and implores him with tears and prayers (LCP ch. 24). For his part, Cuthbert has no quarrel with the secular authority. In neither *Life* does he stand against kings or prophetically judge their actions. The very kings with whom Wilfrid was never reconciled--Ecgfrith and Aldfrith--Cuthbert never angers. In Bede's writings, a mutual friendliness nearly always characterizes relations between the Northumbrian kings and those bishops molded in the Ionan and Lindisfarne tradition. King Oswine humbles himself before Aidan, promising to let the bishop do whatever he wants with the money Oswine has given him; Aidan, in turn, reveres Oswine, crying bitterly when he foresees the King's imminent death (EH 3.14). Bede reports that the Lindisfarne monks would not accept lands or possessions to build monasteries "unless compelled to by the secular authorities" (EH 3.26). This obedient submission to secular authority contrasts sharply with Wilfrid's continued appeals to Rome against it. In the world of Stephen's *Life*, Satan singles out the king as his agent for sowing discord. In the world of both of the Cuthbert *Lives*, the king and the holy man always enjoy harmonious relations.

Two Types of Episcopal Authority: Personal and Official

The two different styles of sanctity associated with Cuthbert and Wilfrid correspond to two different styles of episcopal leadership. The

Hiberno-Saxon tradition that Cuthbert represents regarded elevation to the episcopal rank as far less an honor than did the Latin Mediterranean tradition of Rome and Lyon. Concerning the bishop in the Irish tradition, one authority remarks, "the monastic concept of his office was that he should be a saint rather than a ruler"--a "saint," that is, in the ascetic, monastic mold (Ryan 190). Early Irish Christians respected their bishop not because he wielded a visible authority, but because he willingly and humbly submitted himself to a rigorous monastic routine which demanded of him near-heroic feats of self-renunciation. His authority rested in the charisma that his self-denying lifestyle generated.

The special history and demographics of early medieval Ireland gave rise to this unique understanding of the episcopal office. Because the administrative center of the Irish church was the monastery rather than the diocese, the abbot wielded more authority than the bishop.14 The bishop, a monk who typically served under the abbot, discharged routine ecclesiastical functions among the people who lived on monastery lands. These duties included ordaining clergy, confirming the laity, blessing holy oils, consecrating altars and churches, and other appropriate episcopal functions (Ryan 179). Under this arrangement, the bishop had very little authority attached to his office and no fixed diocese. This mode of ecclesiastical governance seems to have prevailed in early Lindisfarne as well as sixth-century Ireland (LCP ch. 16; EH 4.25).

As bishop, Cuthbert wielded immense authority, but not by virtue of his office. His authority derived rather from his personal charisma, and that, in turn, derived from his ascetic humility. Becoming bishop changed nothing. As the author of the *Anonymous Life* remarks,

> For [as bishop] he continued with the utmost constancy to be what he had been before; he showed the same humility of heart, the same poverty of dress, and, being full of authority and grace, he maintained the dignity of a bishop without abandoning the ideal of the monk or the virtue of the hermit. (LCA 4.1, quoting Sulpicius Severus *Life of St. Martin* 10)

---

14 Sometimes abbots functioned as bishops, sometimes they were only priests. No greater repute seems to have accrued to abbot-bishops than to abbot-priests. If anything, the opposite may have been the case. See Ryan 189.

In addition, his episcopal authority seems neither to have amplified nor diminished his apostolic and prophetic powers as healer and seer.15 Whether bishop at Lindisfarne, guest-master at Ripon, prior at Melrose, or hermit on Farne, Cuthbert is consistently depicted as a holy man in the ascetic mold.

Unlike Cuthbert, Wilfrid is depicted as undergoing a significant change once he begins to exercise his episcopal authority. In chapters 2-14, Stephen presents Wilfrid as meek, humble, and obedient in every way. Beginning with Wilfrid's restoration to the see at York, however, and continuing through to his break with King Ecgfrith (chs. 15-24), Stephen's narrative turns Wilfrid into a man of power who, for the first time, builds and repairs churches (chs. 16, 17, 22), receives gifts of land for the church (ch. 17), resuscitates the dead and dying (chs. 18, 23), instructs the sons of nobles, and gives bounteous gifts to clergy and laity (ch. 21).

Although Stephen's Wilfrid admires the ascetic's qualities and even cultivates them to a certain extent in himself, he seems to understand that his episcopal office requires much more of him than the cultivation of ascetic virtue. The bishops that the historical Wilfrid observed at Rome and Lyon in the 650s wielded immense worldly power and wealth. However much charisma they possessed in their persons, they labored arduously and even suffered death in order to ground religious authority in a charisma that rested not in persons, but in such suprapersonal institutions as church, episcopacy, priesthood, and canon law.16 Although these suprapersonal

---

15 Here, as in other early Christian texts that extol the ascetic type as the highest form of Christlike imitation, there seems to be some suspicion that the episcopal honor might diminish ascetic virtue and the wonder-working power that goes with it. St. Martin, whose image Cuthbert faithfully replicates in many ways, is said by his own admission to have performed fewer miracles as bishop than when he was simply a monk (Sulpicius Severus, *Dialogues* 1.2.4, in Hoare 106). For a good discussion of these issues in relation to the St. Martin material, see Stancliffe 232f.

16 The investment of charisma in the episcopal office can be seen, for example, in some of Constantine's decrees. See, for example, ch. 4 (above), note 27. Following Edward Shils, I understand charisma as accruing in attenuated form to institutions, not simply--as Max Weber would have it--to creative and innovative individuals. To quote Shils, "It seems to be that an attenuated, mediated, institutionalized charismatic propensity is present in the routine functioning of society. There is, in society, a widespread disposition to attribute charismatic

institutions do not inspire or attract in the same way that a single charismatic person might, history has shown that they have helped offer the church a firmer foundation by which it has been able to withstand internal and external assaults upon it. Because there is no guarantee that the church will, in every generation, give birth to such extraordinarily charismatic figures as Cuthbert or Aidan or that it will forever enjoy the cooperation of secular rulers, the survival of the church as a social institution requires that it invest itself in an authority which can withstand the ravages of time and time's unforeseeable vicissitudes.17

The historical Wilfrid was trying to establish just such an authority on which the young English churches could rest. In both Rome and Lyon he had been made acutely aware of the kinds of blows which the church could suffer at the hands of kings, queens and emperors. As a consequence, Wilfrid understood episcopal authority as residing more in the bishop's office, into which a bishop-elect has been consecrated canonically, than in the bishop's person. Such a conception of episcopal authority had vast implications for the way a bishop carried out his teaching and other functions. It is evident that for the anonymous monk of Lindisfarne Cuthbert taught more by his immediate example than by the verbal transmission of a faith defined formally by the ecumenical councils. Apart from the simple statement that Cuthbert preached the Word of God, the *Anonymous Life* indicates nothing about the precise doctrinal content of his preaching and teaching.

By contrast, Stephen states explicitly what Wilfrid taught. Besides offering rudimentary instruction in his preaching (chs. 26, 41), Wilfrid taught the proper observance of Easter (ch. 10), gave King Alhfrith a sermon on peace (ch. 7), brought the Benedictine *Rule* to Northumbria and instructed his monks in the use of a double choir (ch. 47), confessed the orthodox faith

properties to ordinary secular roles, institutions, symbols, and strata or aggregates of persons. Charisma not only disrupts social order; it also maintains or conserves it" (120).

17 To note the importance of such institutions in safeguarding the church's worldly existence does not necessarily imply a positive evaluation of them. Since its beginnings, the Christian tradition has produced those who have been wary of identifying the church's worldly security with its spiritual health. To such as these, the flourishing of the institutional church is seen to occur often at the expense of the gospel. For an early example of this conflict, see Ernst Käsemann's "Paul and Early Catholicism," especially pp. 249-250.

for all of the British Isles in Rome (ch. 53), and perhaps most importantly of all, transmitted to the English churches the rudiments of canon law as he learned them in Rome and perhaps Lyon.18   For Wilfrid, the teaching function of a bishop included more than offering himself as a personal example of piety. It meant teaching and living obediently in accordance with God's law as that law manifested itself in Scripture, the fathers, the canons of the ecclesiastical councils, and other forms of established tradition.   So conceived, such teaching activity presupposed that the bishop had a substantial amount of technical knowledge at his disposal.

Through this kind of teaching, Wilfrid was aiming, as Stephen sees it, to provide for the church of Christ and protect it from the evils of heresy, schism, and persecution. Especially important in this regard was knowledge of canon law, or in Stephen's words, the "rules of ecclesiastical discipline" which Wilfrid learned on his first pilgrimage to Rome.   As chapter four showed, the Roman church of the mid-seventh century held unswervingly to the established canons of Chalcedon and the other authoritative councils in their fight against the emperor and Monotheletism. No less than Rome, Lyon had a strong tradition of canon law. It has been suggested that the first systematically organized collection of canon law in the West, the *Collectio Vetus Gallica*, was compiled and edited in Lyon in about 600 (Mordek 78-79). The Lyonese church's metropolitan status as well as Lyon's old political status as the chief Roman city in Gaul made it a likely center for canon law. In addition, the archbishop of Lyon had at his disposal one of the most prolific *scriptoria* in early medieval Europe. In those manuscripts believed to have been written in Lyon's early scriptorium, E. A. Lowe found two works on canon law (Lowe 17; Coville 507).

The historical Wilfrid probably thought that the proper observance of canon law would help preserve the sometimes precarious unity of the church. As a youth, he doubtless had seen that unity jeopardized in the Easter

---

18 Although Stephen states that Wilfrid first went to Rome to "learn the rules of ecclesiastical discipline" (ch. 4), he seldom depicts Wilfrid explicitly teaching those rules and canons except at the Synod of Whitby (ch. 10). Nevertheless, Wilfrid's repeated appeals to Rome and his conveyance of papal bulls to Northumbria themselves should count as attempts to teach canon law (e.g., chs. 34, 57-58).

controversy at Lindisfarne (EH 3.25); he saw it endangered again at Rome in the 650s during the Monothelete controversy; and perhaps again in Burgundian Gaul, near Lyon, where the emergence of independent Columbanan monasteries and lay-controlled *eigenkirchen* threatened to diminish episcopal control over the Burgundian church and to sever the church of Lyon from its ancient heritage and from its communion with the larger church (Ewig, "Milo" 209-210). Finally, Wilfrid had seen ecclesiastical unity endangered in Northumbria where Ecgfrith's and Aldfrith's refusal to abide by the rules of ecclesiastical discipline threatened the integrity of the episcopal office, and with it, the catholicity and purity of the church. As the eschatological community which recalls the concord between human beings in Eden and foreshadows peace among the saints in eternity, the church cannot signify God's miraculous overcoming of sin and estrangement if it participates in that estrangement itself. Hence the importance of its purity and unity which the ecclesiastical canons and rules of discipline are intended to preserve.

The most enduring symbols of the difference between Wilfrid and Cuthbert still exist today on the Northumbrian landscape. On the one hand, the curious visitor may visit the original crypts in Wilfrid's churches at Ripon and Hexham. On the other, a trip to Lindisfarne will yield little evidence, if any at all, of its seventh-century church. No wonder. The "suitable" episcopal church which Finan built when he was bishop from 651 to 661 was not built to last. As Bede reports, it was constructed in the "Irish fashion" with hewn oak, and thatched with reeds. In this enterprise as in so many others at Lindisfarne, ascetic modesty prevailed.19 Aidan, Cuthbert, and the other Lindisfarne bishops of the seventh century doubtless would have approved of Finan's modest design.

By contrast, Wilfrid expended enormous amounts to erect and decorate his more enduring, magnificent stone churches at Ripon and Hexham. Stephen reports of the Hexham church that no house on the north side of the Alps was built on such a grand scale (LW ch. 22). Unlike his episcopal brothers at Lindisfarne, Wilfrid managed to unite a personally

19 EH 3.25; See Kendrick 2:294.

124

ascetic lifestyle with a public image as bishop which enabled him to wield extraordinary power over his immense ecclesiastical territory. As the previous chapter noted, certain bishops in Rome and Lyon also knew this distinction between private piety and public image. Pope Honorius, for example, adopted a monastic lifestyle in the manner of Gregory the Great, and yet unlike Gregory spent a fortune erecting new churches in Rome and restoring old ones. Behind such elaborate building plans lies a strongly sacramental understanding of the physical church structure itself. According to that understanding, the church and its decor function as earthly windows opening up to the heavenly realm: the stone walls of the physical church recall the invisible church's fortress-like character and its rock-solid apostolic foundation, against which the powers of death will not prevail; the gold and silver that gild the martyr's shrine signify the martyr's dazzling merits, through which Satan's mischief is confounded.[20]

Stephen and Wilfrid doubtless saw the church building through the same sacramental lens. Stephen writes that just as Moses built the wondrous tabernacle of God "to stir up the faith of the people of Israel," so did Wilfrid erect the church at Ripon, adorning her fairly with gold, silver, and varied purples (LW ch. 17). Whereas some might be able to contemplate the bountiful largess of the Creator or the shining virtues of the saints without the aid of physical images, Wilfrid knew that the average lay person could not. As a good *pius pater*, he knew that his flock needed the milk of faith before the solid food, and so he gave it to them by decorating his churches with arrestingly beautiful symbols of the divine majesty and of the communion of saints. In his building of churches, as in his teaching of ecclesiastical discipline, Wilfrid showed a constant concern to establish vital links between the members of his flock and that cloud of witnesses--the prophets, apostles, and martyrs--who had lived, worked, and suffered for the sake of Christ and Christ's church. By dedicating his churches at Ripon and Hexham to Sts. Peter and Andrew, the apostles whom he "especially loved,"

---

20 An inscription from the church of St. Agnes, built by Honorius, reads: "This decorated church of the virgin [Agnes] glistens with various metals, but the virgin, who shines brighter, glistens with her abundant merits even more" (Rossi, *Inscriptiones* 63, 89, 104, 137, as quoted in LP ch. 72 (Honorius), p. 325, n.7).

Wilfrid probably recalled to his flock the suffering and persecution which
Christian discipleship required in the apostolic age and thereby reminded
them of the sacrifice which they might be asked to make (cf. LW ch. 35).

Of course, these magnificent churches were bought at a hefty price.
Not only did they exact a heavy toll from Wilfrid's episcopal treasury, they
also involved risks which some pastors were not willing to take. The gold and
silver ornamentation that a Roman-styled bishop like Wilfrid or Pope
Honorius displayed routinely in their churches, Cuthbert or Aidan would
have regarded as temptation rather than aid to worship. For although an
ornate church and its trappings ought to function as signs for deeper
mysteries to be pondered, they all too often attract worship to themselves.
Even when they function properly as signs, they may signify one thing at the
expense of another. A golden or jeweled cross, for example, may signify the
future glorification of the believer so well that it obscures the suffering and
death which the symbol of the cross essentially represents and to which all
disciples are continually called. In their rejection of such icons,
Northumbria's bishops of the Hiberno-Ionan tradition reveal once again the
immediate and charismatic nature of their ministry. Whereas Wilfrid sees
ecclesiastical offices, institutions, icons, and tradition as the conduits through
which God chooses to save a sinful humanity, Cuthbert calls attention more
immediately to himself, or rather, to the Christ who lives within him, as the
place where the saving power of God most powerfully manifests itself. In the
words of Bede, "Those things which [Cuthbert] taught as needful of doing, he
taught first by doing himself" (LCP ch. 26).

Sanctity and the Problem of Heroism

The intervening thirteen hundred or so years have made it clear which
of these two saints has been the more beloved. Although Wilfrid enjoyed a
respectable cult throughout the rest of the Middle Ages, it hardly compared
to Cuthbert's. Cuthbert's body now rests in a place of honor behind the altar
at Durham Cathedral, and his relics nearby. By contrast, Wilfrid's body has
been consigned to oblivion, some claiming that his remains were translated

to Canterbury in the tenth century, others that they remained at Ripon.21 No remains definitely associated with him survive except for his crypts at Hexham and Ripon. We could wish that the magnificent gospel book which he commissioned for the dedication of the Ripon church had survived; instead we are left with the gospel book commissioned in Cuthbert's memory, the Lindisfarne gospels. Fortunately, Stephen's *Life of Wilfrid* was left for posterity, but just barely. It survives in only two English manuscripts, whereas the *Anonymous Life of Cuthbert* survives at least partially in seven, and Bede's *Prose Life* in thirty-six (Colgrave, *Two Lives* 43-45). If degree of sanctity could be determined by vote, Cuthbert would win overwhelmingly.

From a theological point of view, however, Cuthbert's emergence as the saint beloved of the crowd raises some problems. For if one measure of sanctity in the early medieval period had to do with how well one's experience mirrored the Christ-like experience of the apostles, then the debate about sanctity--which the crowd has settled by its decided preference for Cuthbert--should in fact remain open. It should do so because it seems to have been settled without sufficient consideration for Scripture's testimony about the distinguishing marks of the apostolic and Christ-like experience. As the beginning of this chapter showed, the author of the *Anonymous Life of Cuthbert* implies that those distinguishing marks are to be found in the apostles' abilities to foresee the future, heal the sick, and perform other miracles. This picture of the apostle as a wonder-worker and seer has as its New Testament prototype the image of the apostle as sketched by the author of Luke-Acts. In this respect, the apostles are shown to continue the wonder-working aspects of Jesus' earthly ministry.

The apostle Paul, agreeing with the author of Luke-Acts, indicates that a true apostle does indeed work signs and wonders, but insists that there is more to the apostolic experience than simply this (2 Cor. 12.12). For Paul, to be an apostle also means to suffer and to manifest human weakness in an

---

21 Eadmer's *Life of Wilfrid* relates that Archbishop Odo of Canterbury (d. 959) translated Wilfrid's remains from Ripon to Canterbury (ch. 57). According to the Ripon Psalter, however, Archbishop Gray translated Wilfrid's body at Ripon in 1224 (Fowler 49). In the notes for his edition of the Wilfrid *Life*, Colgrave relates that some northerners claimed that Odo took the body not of Wilfrid I, but of Wilfrid II to Canterbury (186-187).

especially acute way. Writing to the church at Corinth, he explains, "For I think that God has exhibited us apostles as last of all, like men sentenced to death; because we have become a spectacle to the world, to angels and to men" (1 Cor. 4.9). Like Christ, the apostle does indeed live under a death sentence, and Paul interprets that sentence in its broadest possible sense. In accordance with the predominant understanding of the earliest Cuthbert *Lives*, such a death sentence includes the apostle's experience of physical want and bodily deprivation--the kind of evil which assaults human life on a purely bodily level: "To the present hour we hunger and thirst, we are ill-clad and buffeted and homeless, and we labor, working with our own hands" (1 Cor. 4.11a). In accordance with the predominant understanding of the *Life of Wilfrid*, however, that sentence also includes persecution and other evils which human life suffers in its purely social aspect. The true apostle knows this kind of evil only too well. For Paul, to suffer such evil is a hallmark of the apostolic vocation and establishes his authority over and against certain false apostles:

> Are they servants of Christ? I am a better one--I am talking like a madman--with far greater labors, far more imprisonments, with countless beatings, and often near death. Five times I have received at the hands of the Jews the forty lashes less one. Three times I have been beaten with rods; once I was stoned. (2 Cor. 11.23-25a)

Through the power of God, however, the apostle who experiences that evil finds also that it is overcome: "When reviled, we bless; when persecuted, we endure; when slandered, we try to conciliate; we have become, and are now, as the refuse of the world, the off-scouring of all things" (1 Cor. 4.12b-13).

Although Paul may not argue that persecution is the most fundamental form of apostolic suffering, he would surely assert that persecution belongs essentially to it. On this point the author of Luke-Acts would certainly agree and, as we have shown, so would Stephen the priest.22

---

22 Examples of apostolic persecution in the book of Acts abound: Peter and John are imprisoned (4.3, 5.18-19); the apostles are flogged (5.40); the Jews plot to kill Paul (9.23, 9.29-30, 23.12-15); Herod beheads James, brother of John, and imprisons Peter (12.1-5); the Jews persecute Paul and Barnabas in Antioch (13.50-51); Paul and Barnabas are persecuted at Iconium (14.5-6) and at Lystra (14.19-20); Paul and Silas are stripped and flogged in Phillipi (16.19-24); Paul is seized and beaten in Jerusalem (21.30-36).

Persecution for these authors is nothing of which to be ashamed. It is a present type of future hopeless or death-like situations--situations like bodily death and, more importantly, the Last Judgment. Like persecution, these future events involve the experiencing of an evil which seems to invalidate God's eternally valid promise of blessing. As such, they call for radical faith and hope.

Although Cuthbert is shown to experience various death-like or cross-like situations, they never come in the form of persecution. On the contrary, both the anonymous author and Bede depict Cuthbert as universally beloved. He never quarrels with kings; he never gives offense; he is never despised. However attractive Cuthbert's geniality may be on one level, it could be regarded as theologically suspect on another. As we have just shown, major New Testament authors, including Paul and the Luke-Acts author, associate closely Christlikeness and persecution. To become Christlike, therefore, is to be despised, to become a curse and a stumbling-block for unbelievers (Gal. 3.13; 1 Cor. 1.23). It is to fulfill, as Christ did, the type of the Suffering Servant, who "was despised and rejected by men," or to become like the author of Psalm 21, who is scorned and mocked by all (Is. 53.3; Vg Ps. 21.7-8).

Whereas Stephen depicts Wilfrid as fulfilling this type in every way, the anonymous author seems never to depict Cuthbert as scandalous in anyone's eyes. Having become the object of everyone's admiration and no one's scorn, he came to be regarded both by his own circle and by the many adherents of his later medieval cult as the extraordinary Christian who, by virtue of his ascetic heroism, saves ordinary Christians from disease and death. Since Cuthbert was portrayed in this way, one might wonder--as it seems Stephen and Wilfrid's *familia* did--whether Cuthbert's experience authentically approximates Christ's or the apostles'. For in addition to healing and saving, Christ and the apostles call all who have ears to hear them, not just the ascetic heroes, to judgment, repentance, and discipleship. From Stephen's viewpoint, just as Christ and the apostles willingly subjected themselves to the hatred and persecution of the crowd and became an offense and a stumbling block to their hearers, so must all who confess God's saving work in Christ do the same.

While Stephen does not call into question the ascetic vocation as such, his emphasis on Wilfrid's persecution exposes the ascetic's temptation to choose his own form of suffering, namely, that of self-imposed deprivation. By so choosing, the ascetic forestalls God's own choice, a choice which may dictate persecution instead. Such forestalling is, however, a potential danger rather than a certain flaw of asceticism. Stephen would certainly have agreed with Kierkegaard's observation that the medieval ascetic understood what most others do not: that Christian discipleship demands a radical renunciation of will. Yet Kierkegaard, and probably Stephen too, was highly suspicious of the praise that the crowd lavished upon the ascetic. For he worried that such praise would drown out the call of radical renunciation which God addresses to the single individual. In addition, it might obscure the element of offense and scandal so central to Christian discipleship:

> The defect of medieval asceticism was that it drew a line through [denied the validity of] specifically Christian suffering, that is, suffering at the hands of men. The ascetic permitted men to admire him for being extraordinary. Thus after all, numbers entered into the matter, for it was numbers of men who represented ordinary Christianity. If the ascetic had said, what is the truth, "There is no such thing as extraordinary Christians. What my life expresses is just an approximation to what is demanded of us all, an approximation to quite simply being a Christian"--then he would have been persecuted. (Kierkegaard 359)

Cuthbert well may have done what Kierkegaard thought it necessary for him to do, namely, denounced the crowd's adoration of him, called its members to a life of renunciation no less radical than his, thus making them uneasy, envious, and angry. If he did, the anonymous author never tells us so. For the latter, many factors contribute to Cuthbert's sanctity, but persecution is not one of them.

Stephen's depiction of Wilfrid as a saint offers such a stark contrast to this earliest depiction of Cuthbert that one wonders if Stephen did not make that contrast purposefully. That contrast reveals not simply nor even primarily a difference in partisan loyalties. It has to do more with enduring religious questions about who God is, about how God becomes manifest in human life, and about the sham and authentic ways by which God may be

130

worshipped and served. Taken together, these two *Lives* exhibit a debate about sanctity.

Responding to the anonymous author, Stephen asserts that persecution belongs essentially to the Christlike and apostolic life. Perhaps more importantly, he affirms that a radical obedience is required of all who would be Christ's disciples, and not just of an ascetic elite. For Stephen that obedience is made visible in one's willingness to obey, as Mercia's good king Aethilred put it, "every jot and tittle" of God's law as that law had been delivered in Christ to Peter and the apostles, and through them to the apostolic church of Rome, which preserves that law unspotted through her preaching and her canons (LW ch. 57). In accordance with good Matthean theology, Stephen affirms that discipleship requires not the relaxation of this law, but its fulfillment. Its diligent observance should extend to the monastery, and far beyond. At one end of the spectrum, it should extend to kings, queens, archbishops and other temporal lords for whom such radical obedience is scandalous, since they have chosen to become lords for themselves; on the other end, it should extend to such ordinary folk as the woman who, having experienced firsthand God's radical goodness through Wilfrid's healing of her son, sought exemption from the radical obedience which that goodness demands (LW ch. 18).

With the kings and with the woman, modern readers of Stephen's *Life* have tended to feel uneasy in Wilfrid's presence. Perhaps medieval readers did also. At one level, along with such historians as R. L. Poole, John Inett, and Thomas Carte, moderns distrust the uncritical acceptance that Wilfrid seems to have inspired in his hagiographer. They sense that a scoundrel lurks behind Stephen's literary portrait. Yet at another level, the uneasiness that moderns experience may have less to do with their dislike of Stephen's distorted portrait than with certain religious convictions expressed in the *Life* that conflict with their own.

For example, against the modern conviction that the good life is self-chosen, that it consists largely in the individual's autonomy and self-determination, Stephen's Wilfrid insists that the good life consists in a radical obedience to God that manifests itself concretely in obedience to certain human individuals and institutions which God, through Christ, has invested with divine authority. More significantly, against the modern conviction that the true hallmark of sanctity, like that of heroism, is its ability to win for the saint the crowd's affection, Stephen's Wilfrid reminds readers of his *Life* that Christ, the prophets, apostles, martyrs and confessors were better acquainted with scorn and derision than with popularity and approbation. As it was for them, so must it be for all who are chosen for discipleship.

Modern readers of Stephen's *Life* often have taken offense at what they perceive to have been Wilfrid's scoundrel and selfish attempts to win back his episcopal jurisdiction over the entire Northumbrian diocese. However justified their offense may be, it may serve to distract readers from the even more offensive challenge that Wilfrid's life of exile and persecution issues to those who rest secure in the good opinion that others have of them. Like the medieval followers of Cuthbert's cult, moderns too are tempted to venerate only those saints whose sanctity manifests itself in popular, conventional, and undisturbing ways. Against that temptation stands Stephen's offensive and sometimes haunting depiction of sanctity. For modern readers of Stephen's *Life*, that depiction ever tries to subvert a conventional sense of sanctity and to inspire, through a saint who scandalizes, a radical faith of obedience that patiently hopes for a future glory amidst present tribulations.

APPENDIX I: Structural Outline of Stephen's *Life of Bishop Wilfrid*

(NOTE: Numbers in brackets indicate chapter numbers.
The chapter numbers in parentheses after chapter 60
indicate the chapter numbering in the Colgrave edition.)

I. **PREDESTINED:** Called by God in the womb; signs at birth   **[1]**

II. **CALLED:** Wilfrid's Preparation as Apostle to the English   **[2-23]**

   A. **The Call Proper**

      1. **Divinely Inspired--**

         a. With divine help, Wilfrid finds favor in
           Queen Eanflaed's sight.   **[2]**

         b. At the suggestion of the Holy Spirit, Wilfrid
           desires to visit the see of the Apostle Peter.   **[3]**

         c. God assists Wilfrid through the good offices
           of Dalfinus.   **[4]**

      2. **Content--**

         a. to visit the Apostolic See
         b. to learn the rules of ecclesiastical discipline

      3. **Purpose**--that England might grow in serving God.

B. **Preparation for the Call**

    1. in its **monastic** aspect--

        a. at Lindisfarne--learned psalter and several books,
            sought to live the monastic life in humility
            and obedience   [2]
        b. at Canterbury--learned psalter after the Roman use   [3]

    2. in its **priestly (and episcopal)** aspect--   [5]

        a. acquired a mind to read and an eloquence to teach the
            Gospels
        b. prayed at the shrines of saints in Rome
        c. learned from Boniface the four Gospels perfectly,
            the Easter Rule, and other rules of
            ecclesiastical discipline

    3. by **encountering danger in Gaul**--   [6]

        a. learns "many things"
        b. receives tonsure from Dalfinus
        c. encounters grave danger and becomes a confessor

C. **Confirmation of the Call** through initial successes as abbot,
     priest, and bishop   [7-23]

    1. becomes abbot at Ripon   [8]

    2. ordained priest   [9]

    3. succeeds at the Synod of Whitby   [10]

    4. consecrated bishop   [11-15]

    5. builds magnificent churches   [16-17, 22]

    6. performs miracles   [13(?), 18, 23]

    7. makes King Ecgfrith successful in battle   [19-20]

APPENDIX II: References and Allusions to Wilfrid as Biblical Type in Stephen's *Life of Wilfrid*

(NOTE: Chapter Numbers in this Appendix reflect the numbering in the Levison edition)

TYPE	NAME	CHAPTER	PAGE Levison/Colgrave	SOURCE	NEAR TYPE
Patriarch					
	Abraham	4	197.16/10	Gen. 12.1	
	---	35	229.16/72	---	Exile
	Jacob	3	196.12/8	Gen. 28.1	
		64	259.29/140	Gen. 49.28	
		2	194.28/6	Gen. 49.28	
	Jacob's sons	2	194.28/6	Gen. 49.28	
	Joseph	42	235.18/84	Gen. 41	
Prophet					
	---	8	202.8/18	---	
	Moses	13	207.20/26	Ex. 10.20	
		13	208.6/28	Ex. 17.12&v.10;	
		17	211.15/34	Ex. 25.9&c	
		35	229.19/72	---	
	Aaron	35	229.19/72	---	
	Samuel	2	195.15/6	1 Sam. 3.1	
		16	211.7/34	1 Sam. 2.30	
	Jonathan	57	252.12/124	1 Sam. 14.27	

TYPE	NAME	CHAPTER	PAGE Levison/Colgrave	SOURCE	NEAR TYPE
Prophet (continued)					
	David	7	201.20/16	1 Sam. 18.1	
		9	202.21/18	--	
		15	210.6/32	1 Sam. 24.6	
	Elijah	24	218.10/48	1 Kg. 18.4	
	Elijah/	18	213.7/38	---	Wonder-
	Elisha	23	217.21/46	1 Kg. 17.21 cf. 2 Kg. 4.34	Worker
	Ezekiel	11	205.14/24	Ezek. 1.1	
	Jeremiah	11	94.4/4	Jer. 1.5	
	Daniel	16	210.21/34	Dan. 7.15	
	John the Baptist	11	205.14/24	Lk. 3.23 cf. 1.36, 56	Confessor
		41	234.15/82	Mt. 3.2,28.19, Acts 2.38	Christ/ Apostle
Christ					
	---	39	232.2/78	Mt. 27.19	
	---	66	262.5/144	Mk. 16.5	
	---	35	229.22/72	[NT]	Disciples
Apostle					
	Andrew	67	262.30/146	---	
	John	6	200.5/14	Pseudo-Abdias 20	
		44	239.6/90	Pseudo-Abdias 2	
		37	230.24/74	Rev 1.9	Evangelist
	Paul	31	97.3/8	Acts 15.36-39	
		51	98.5/12	Gal. 2.1-2	
		14	209.14/30	Acts 14.26	
		24	219.7/50	Acts 25.11	
		23	217.20/46	Acts 20.10	Wonder- Worker

TYPE	NAME	CHAPTER	PAGE Levison/Colgrave	SOURCE	NEAR TYPE
Apostle (continued)					
	[Paul]	26	220.16/52	1 Cor. 3.10	
	Paul and Barnabas	5	198.20/12	Acts 13.3	
	Peter	36	230.13/74	Acts 12.7	
		41	234.23/82	Acts 10.44-48	
		67	262.30/146	---	
		38	231.22/76	Acts 12.7	Evangelist
		25	219.24/50	Acts 12.11	Christ
	---	38	231.23/76	---	Baptizer
	---	18	213.7/38	Mt. 10.1	Wonder-Worker
Confessor					
	---	8	201.23/16	LW ch. 6	
Exile					
	---	40	232.23/40	---	
	---	43	236.9/86	---	
Miscellaneous Types					
Angel of God		7	201.13/16	---	
Israel		35	229.16/72	Ps. 104.13	Exile
Esther		41	234.21/82	Est. 2.9	
King Hezekiah		56	252.5/122	2 Kg. 20.6	
Suffering Servant		36	229.31/72	Is. 53.7	
victim of persecution		38	231.24/76	Heb. 10.32-33	Suffering Servant, Apostle
Christ's disciples		35	229.22/72	[NT]	Christ

APPENDIX III: Indexes of Scripture and Patristic Sources in the *Life of Bishop Wilfrid*

In this Index, all boldfaced entries denote direct or nearly direct citations of Scripture. Citations in parentheses indicate one scriptural passage cited by another. All other entries indicate allusions to the scriptural passage. All page and chapter references are based on Levison's MGH edition. Citations from the Psalms are numbered in accordance with the Vulgate. To find the corresponding Psalm in the RSV, NEB or other English versions of Scripture, simply augment the number of the Vulgate Psalm by one for all Psalms after Psalm 9.

Most of these references can be found in the margins of the Levison edition. When citing a reference to one of the synoptic gospels, Levison had the tendency to list only the reference in Matthew, omitting exact or near parallels in Mark and Luke. The index below cites these Markan and Lukan parallels.

Scripture and Patristic Works to LW--

Each entry below contains three columns. The first is the biblical chapter and verse; the second is the chapter number in Levison; the third is the page and line number in Levison where the citation or allusion occurs.

Gen.

12.1	4	197.16
18.10	4	197.20
18.10	63	259.3
18.10	34	228.26
18.10	48	243.15
24.40	41	234.3
27.4	43	238.8
28.1	2	194.28
28.1	3	196.12
38.26	33	228.20
41.13	57	252.19
41.13	1	194.17
41.13	67	263.15
41.14	37	231.1

Gen.

(48.15)	64	259.29
49.28	2	194.28
(49.28)	64	259.29

Ex.

3.2	1	194.12
10.20	13	207.20
14.13	1	194.11
14.21	13	206.15
14.21	7	200.12
17.12	13	208.6
25.9	17	211.15
26.1	17	211.15
36.8	17	211.15

142

Ex.				**2 Chr.**			
	41.14	42	235.17		24	19	214.10
	47.29	43	238.6				
	48.15	2	194.28	**Est.**			
Num.					**2.9**	2	195.2
	22.5	24	218.18		2.9	41	234.21
	22.12	24	218.18	**Pr.**			
	22.41	13	207.23		14.13	61	257.11
	23.27	13	207.23				
	28.14	3	196.8	**Ps.**			
Dt.					**19.6**	67	263.18
	10.19	28	222.3		21.22	18	213.21
	16.19	24	218.17		**26.13**	32	227.13
	17.11	53	247.14		(43.22)	36	229.31
	34.7	13	208.2		**44.14**	17	211.14
Jg.					44.15	17	211.14
	4	20	215.17		**50.9**	16	211.3
	7.7	13	207.29		60.4	30	224.31
	8.10	13	207.29		67.36	30	263.13
1 Sam.					**67.36**	60	257.3
	1.10	18	213.13		**67.36**	18	213.6
	2.30	16	211.7		70.3	30	224.31
	3.1	2	195.15		72.28	22	216.22
	5	39	232.13		103.30	64	259.33
	5	34	229.11		**104.13**	35	229.18
	14.27	57	252.12		**104.21f.**	42	235.18
	15.22	32	227.16		**104.21**	42	236.1
	16.12-13	9	202.22		**120.8**	33	228.18
	17.49	13	207.25		138.17	13	208.14
	18.1	7	201.20	**Is.**			
	24.7	15	210.6		**(53.7)**	36	229.31
1 Kg.					66.2	28	222.2
	8	17	211.25	**Jer.**			
	8.22	17	211.29		**1.5**	1	194.4
	12	33	228.8		1.5	36	230.10
	17	18	213.7		31.26	56	251.31
	17.21	23	217.21		31.26	61	257.29
	18.4	24	218.10	**Ezek.**			
	18.4	6	199.17		1.1	11	205.14
2 Kg.				**Dan.**			
	4	18	213.7		**7.15**	16	210.21
	4.34	23	217.21				
	20.2	56	252.8				
	20.6	56	252.5				
	20.9	56	251.24				

Am.

9.4	4	197.8

Mt.

3.2	41	234.15
5.15	1	194.15
8.5	37	230.30
8.15	37	231.6
9.20	65	261.24
10.1	18	213.9
10.12	7	201.7
11.29	43	238.5
12.42	5	198.7
13.46	8	202.6
14.24	13	207.13
16.18-19	10	204.13
16.19	34	229.4
16.19	29	223.15
16.19	39	232.10
16.19	60	255.21
16.26	28	222.15
18.20	61	257.24
19.29	4	197.19
20.22	6	200.7
21.13	16	210.22
25.33	32	227.13
25.34	32	227.17
27.9	27	220.19
27.19	39	232.2
28.19	41	234.16

Mk.

1.31	37	231.6
5.25f.	65	261.24
6.7	18	213.9
6.48	13	207.13
7.26	18	213.27
8.36	28	222.15
9.23	18	213.25
9.49	7	201.10
10.29-30	4	197.19
10.38	6	200.7
16.5	66	262.6

Lk.

3.23	11	205.14
4.39	37	231.6
7.38	18	213.23
8.43f.	65	261.24
9.1	18	213.9
9.25	28	222.15
11.31	5	198.7
11.33	1	194.15
18.29	4	197.19
19.46	16	210.22
21.19	43	238.4

Jn.

1.9	36	230.9
6.45	2	194.23
14.18	61	257.18
21.21	10	203.11

Acts

2.38	41	234.15
2.41	41	234.24
7.6	33	228.13
8.32	36	229.31
10.44	41	234.23
12.11	25	219.24
12.7	36	230.13
12.7	38	231.22
13.3	5	198.20
14.26	41	234.22
14.26	14	209.14
15.37-39	3	197.3
20.10	23	217.20
25.11	24	219.7

Rom.

8.23	44	238.21
8.29-30	1	194.1
8.36	36	229.31

1 Cor.

3.10	26	220.16
8.7	49	243.25
16.9	41	234.22
16.9	14	209.14

LW to Scripture and Patristic Works

This portion of the Index lists scriptural and patristic citations for each chapter of the LW. In each column, the leftmost item designates the chapter number of the LW, the middle item designates the scriptural or patristic passage cited there, and the rightmost item designates the page and line number in the Levison edition where the citation can be found.

11.	**Tit. 1.7-9**	205.8	18.	**Ps.67.36**	213.6
	1 Tim. 3.3	205.9		1 Kg. 17	213.7
	Lk. 3.23	205.14		2 Kg. 4	213.7
	Ezek. 1.1	205.14		Mt. 10.1	213.9
	LCA 4.1	205.20-30		Mk. 6.7	213.9
	Isidore of Sev.			Lk. 9.1	213.9
	De Eccl. Offic.			1 Sam. 1.10	213.13
	2.5.47	205.20-30		1 Macc 2.60	213.21
				2 Tim. 4.17	213.21
12.	1 Tim. 6.20	207.6		Ps. 21.22	213.21
	2 Tim. 1.6	207.6		Lk. 7.38	213.23
				Mk. 9.23	213.25
13.	Mt. 14.24	207.13		Mk. 7.26	213.27
	Mk. 6.48	207.13			
	Ex. 10.20	207.20	19.	2 Chr. 24	214.10
	Num. 22.41	207.23		2 Macc. 8.18	215.1
	Num. 23.27	207.23			
	1 Sam. 17.49	207.25	20.	Jg. 4	215.17
	Jg. 7.7	207.29			
	Jg. 8.10	207.29	21.	**2 Cor. 6.7**	216.18
	Dt. 34.7	208.2			
	Ex. 17.12	208.6	22.	Ps. 72.28	216.22
	Ps. 138.17	208.14			
	Ex. 14.21	206.15	23.	Acts 20.10	217.20
				1 Kg. 17.21	217.21
14.	1 Cor. 16.9	209.14		2 Kg. 4.34	217.21
	Acts 14.26	209.14			
			24.	1 Pet. 5.8	218.3
15.	1 Th. 5.15	210.5		1 Pet. 3.7	218.6
	1 Sam. 24.7	210.6		1 Kg. 18.4	218.10
				Dt. 16.19	218.17
16.	**Dan. 7.15**	210.21		Num. 22.5	218.18
	Mt. 21.13	210.22		Num. 22.12	218.18
	Lk. 19.46	210.22		Acts 25.11	219.7
	Ps. 50.9	211.3			
	1 Sam. 2.30	211.7	25.	Acts 12.11	219.24
17.	2 Cor. 11.2	211.11			
	Ps. 44.15	211.14	26.	1 Cor. 3.10	220.16
	Ps. 44.14	211.14			
	Ex. 25.9	211.15	27.	Mt. 27.9	220.19
	Ex. 26.1	211.15			
	Ex. 36.8	211.15	28.	Is. 66.2	222.2
	1 Kg. 8	211.25		Dt. 10.19	222.3
	1 Esd. 3.3	211.27		Mk. 8.36	222.15
	1 Kg. 8.22	211.29		Mt. 16.26	
				Lk. 9.25	

29.	Mt. 16.19	223.15		39.	Mt. 27.19	232.2
					Mt. 16.19	232.10
30.	[Wilfrid's petition to Pope Agatho]				1 Sam. 5	232.13
	Ps. 60.4	224.31		40.	---	
	Ps. 70.3	224.31				
				41.	**Gen. 24.40**	234.3
31.	---				1 Pet. 2.2	234.10
					Mt. 3.2	234.15
32.	**Ps. 26.13**	227.13			**Acts 2.38**	234.15
	Mt. 25.33	227.13			Mt. 28.19	234.16
	1 Sam. 15.22	227.16			Est. 2.9	234.21
	Mt. 25.34	227.17			1 Cor. 16.9	234.22
					Acts 14.26	234.22
	1 Kg. 12	228.8			Acts 10.44	234.23
	Acts 7.6	228.13			Acts 2.41	234.24
	Ps. 120.8	228.18				
	Gen. 38.26	228.20		42.	Gen. 41.14	235.17
					Ps. 104.21	236.1
34.	Gen. 18.10	228.26			**Ps. 104.21f.**	235.18
	Mt. 16.19	229.4				
	1 Sam. 5	229.11		43.	[Theodore's letter to	
					Aethilred]	
35.	**Ps. 104.13**	229.18			Lk. 21.19	238.4
	Heb. 12.5-6	229.24			Mt. 11.29	238.5
	Heb. 12.1	229.26			**Gen. 47.29**	238.6
					Gen. 27.4	238.8
36.	**Acts 8.32**	229.31				
	(Is. 53.7)	229.31		44.	Rom. 8.23	238.21
	Rom. 8.36	229.31			*Ps.-Abdias* 5.2	239.5
	(Ps. 43.22)	229.31				
	Jn. 1.9	230.9		45.	---	
	Jer. 1.5	230.10				
	Acts 12.7	230.13		46.	---	
				47.	---	
37.	Rev. 1.9	230.24				
	Mt. 8.5	230.30		48.	Gen. 18.10	243.15
	Gen. 41.14	231.1				
	Mt. 8.15	231.6		49.	1 Cor. 8.7	243.25
	Mk. 1.31	232.6				
	Lk. 4.39	231.6		50.	---	
38.	Acts 12.7	231.22		51.	[Winfrid's petition to John]	
	Heb. 10.32-34	231.24				
				52.	---	

148

53.	Dt. 17.11	247.14
54.	[Pope John's letter to Kings Aethilred and Alfrith]	
55.	Gal. 6.14	251.2
56.	2 Kg. 20.9	251.24
	Jer. 31.26	257.29
	2 Kg. 20.6	252.5
	2 Kg. 20.2	252.8
57.	1 Sam. 14.27	252.12
	Gen. 41.13	252.19
58.	---	
59.	---	
60.	Mt. 16.19	255.21
	Ps. 67.36	257.3
	Tit. 3.7	257.9
61	Pr. 14.13	257.11
	Jn. 14.18	257.18
	Mt. 18.20	257.24
	Jer. 31.26	257.29
62.	---	
63.	Gen. 18.10	259.3
64.	Heb. 11.21	259.29
	(Gen. 48.15)	259.29
	(Gen. 49.28)	259.29
	Ps. 103.30	259.33
65.	**Mt. 9.20**	261.24
	Mk. 5.25f.	261.24
	Lk. 8.43f.	261.24
66.	Mk. 16.5	262.6
67.	Ps. 67.36	263.13
	Gen. 41.13	263.15
	2 Macc. 4.24	263.18
	Ps. 19.6	263.18

APPENDIX IV: A Word Comparison of *Confessor, Prophet* and *Apostle*
in Stephen's *Life of Bishop Wilfrid* and the *Anonymous Life of St. Cuthbert*

I.   **CONFESSOR** (and Martyr)

    A.   The *Anonymous Life of St. Cuthbert* uses *confessor* and *martyr*
in the same generic way which does *not* necessarily connote
persecution:

        1.   *CONFESSOR*:
            a.   **"In honor also of the holy confessor of God** [*In
honore quoque sancti confessoris Dei*]...many
miracles are wrought daily." (4.16)
            b.   "On the Sunday [a man seized with a great
illness] said to a servant of our monastery: 'Take
me...to the place where the **body of the confessor**
[*corpus confessoris*] of God rests.'" (4.16)

        2.   *MARTYR*:
            a.   "And so the Lord, **in honor of the holy martyr**
[*pro honore sancti martyris*] after his death
granted health to many men, according to their
faith." (4.15)
            b.   "I ask the abbot for the shoes which were on the
feet of the holy and incorruptible **martyr of God**
[*martyris Dei*]." (4.17)

    B.   The *Life of Bishop Wilfrid* carefully distinguishes between a
confessor and one who undergoes *martyrium*, but understands
both specifically in connection with persecution:

        1.   "So the holy bishop [Dalfinus] won **a martyr's crown**
[*martyrio coronatus*]; but when St Wilfrid, despoiled and
ready for the prize of martyrdom [*paratus ad palmam
martyrii*], was standing by fearlessly, the dukes asked,
'Who is that handsome young man who is preparing for
death?' 'A foreigner of the English race from Britain'
they were told. Thereupon they said, 'Spare him and do

not touch him.' So now our St. Wilfrid **has become a confessor** [*confessor factus est*] like **John the Apostle** and Evangelist, who sat uninjured in a cauldron of boiling oil and drank deadly poison unharmed." (6)

2. "[King Ecgfrith] ordered that Wilfrid should be kept, though so good a man and so great a bishop, bound hands and feet with fetters, in solitary confinement. So in accordance with the king's command the reeve ordered the smiths to make iron fetters. The smiths, though they had no reason for doing so, entered upon their task with energy, measuring the limbs of **our holy confessor** [*sancti confessoris nostri*]." (38)

II. **PROPHET** (prophesy/prophetic)

A. The Cuthbert *Life* uses the terms which derive from *prophet* (e.g., *prophetic/prophecy*) to connote Cuthbert's power as a seer, and never in connection with suffering or persecution:

1. "Then immediately...Cuthbert described the wonderful vision just as he had seen it, **prophesying further** [*prophetans quoque*] to them that it was the soul of a most holy bishop or of some other great person." (1.5)

2. **"By the prophetic spirit of God** [*prophetali Spiritu Dei*], Cuthbert foresaw the devil tempting them." (2.6)

3. "After **many prophetic words** [*multa verba prophetica*], all of which came to pass without fail, Cuthbert sailed to his own place." (3.6)

B. The Wilfrid *Life* usually understands the word *prophet* and its derivatives in connection with *persecution*:

1. "The Bishop Wilfrid said, '...Moses and Aaron too and **all the prophets of God** [*omnes prophetae Dei*] endured the persecution of man, trusting in the Lord.'" (35)

2. "Immediately this sorceress [Queen Iurminburg] shot poisoned arrows of speech from her quiver into the heart of the king, as the wicked Jezebel did when she slew the **prophets of the Lord** [*prophetas Dei*] and persecuted Elijah." (24)

III. **APOSTLE** (apostolic)

    A.   The Cuthbert *Life* uses the word *apostle* and its derivatives in connection with Cuthbert's healing miracles and his predictive powers, but never with persecution or suffering:

        1.   "Therefore as Saint Cuthbert excelled in virtues in his bishopric, the Lord completely and fully increased the dignity and authority of that office through him by signs and wonders; for what we read concerning the **Apostles,** 'Whatsoever ye shall loose on earth'...was fulfilled in him with respect to things of the soul as well as the body." (4.2)

        2.   "She came breathless into the church...realizing not only that in this matter there was in him [Cuthbert] a **spirit of prophecy** [*prophetiae spiritum*], but also perceiving in all things his **apostolic foresight** [*apostolicam providentiam*]." (4.10)

    B.   The Wilfrid *Life* often associates the apostles (or disciples) with persecution:

        1.   Cf. the comparison with the **apostle John** [I.B.1].

        2.   "But our bishop...sought the judgment of the Apostolic See, as the **Apostle Paul,** when he had been condemned by the Jews without cause, appealed to Caesar." (24)

        3.   "We read also...that Jesus Christ was crucified by the Jews and his **disciples** scattered. Afterwards, throughout the whole world, they and their followers after various temptations received their crown."

WORKS CITED

Ancient and Medieval Sources

Acta [sancti Annemundi] auctore anonymo. Ed. Pierre Chifflet, S.J. Acta Sanctorum--September 7. Paris: Victor Palmé, 1867. [September 28th]. 694-696.

Acts of Andrew. Trans. E. Best. In *New Testament Apocrypha*. Vol. 2. Ed. Edgar Hennecke, Wilhelm Schneemelcher, and R. McL. Wilson. *New Testament Apocrypha*. 2 vols. Philadelphia: Westminster P, 1964. 408-423.

Acts of Paul. Trans. R. McL. Wilson. In *New Testament Apocrypha*. Vol. 2. Ed. Edgar Hennecke, Wilhelm Schneemelcher, and R. McL. Wilson. *New Testament Apocrypha*. 2 vols. Philadelphia: Westminster P, 1964. 352-390.

Acts of Peter. Trans. G. C. Stead. In *New Testament Apocrypha*. Vol. 2. Ed. Edgar Hennecke, Wilhelm Schneemelcher, and R. McL. Wilson. *New Testament Apocrypha*. 2 vols. Philadelphia: Westminster P, 1964. 276-322.

Acts of Thomas. Trans. R. McL. Wilson. In *New Testament Apocrypha*. Vol. 2. Ed. Edgar Hennecke, Wilhelm Schneemelcher, and R. McL. Wilson. *New Testament Apocrypha*. 2 vols. Philadelphia: Westminster P, 1964. 442-531.

Alcuin. *Poem on the Bishops, Kings, and Saints of the Church of York*. In *Alcuin: The Bishops, Kings, and Saints of York*. Ed. and trans. Peter Godman. Oxford Medieval Texts. Oxford: Clarendon P, 1982. 1-135.

Aldhelm. *Aldhelmi Opera*. Ed. Rudolf Ehwald. MGH AA 15. Berlin, 1919.

Ambrose. *Epistola*. PL 16.913-1342. Eng. translation in *Saint Ambrose: Letters*. Trans. Sister Mary Melchior Beyenka, O.P. Fathers of the Church 26. Washington, D.C.: Catholic U of America P, 1954.

Anastasius the Librarian. *Collectanea*. PL 129.557-742.

Anonymous Life of St. Cuthbert. In *Two Lives of St. Cuthbert*. Ed. and trans. Bertram Colgrave. Cambridge: Cambridge UP, 1940. 59-139.

154

Athanasius. *The Life of Antony.* In *Athanasius: The Life of Antony and the Letter to Marcellinus.* Trans. Robert C. Gregg. The Classics of Western Spirituality. New York: Paulist P, 1980.

Augustine. *On Christian Doctrine.* Ed. and Trans. D. W. Robertson, Jr. The Library of the Liberal Arts. Indianapolis: Bobbs, 1958.

_____. *On Rebuke and Grace.* In *St. Augustin: Anti-Pelagian Writings.* Ed. Philip Schaff. Trans. Peter Holmes and Robert Wallis. American Edition. A Select Library of the Nicene and Post-Nicene Fathers (First Series) 5. Grand Rapids, Michigan: Eerdmans, 1987. 471-491.

_____. *Tractates on the Gospel of John.* In *St. Augustin: Homilies on the Gospel of John.* Trans. John Gibb and James Innes. A Select Library of the Nicene and Post-Nicene Fathers (First Series) 7. New York: The Christian Literature Co., 1888. 7- 452.

Bede. *The Ecclesiastical History of the English People.* In *Bede's Ecclesiastical History of the English People.* Ed. and trans. Bertram Colgrave and R. A. B. Mynors. Oxford Medieval Texts. Oxford: Clarendon P, 1969.

_____. *Lives of the Abbots.* In *Venerabilis Bedae Opera Historica.* Vol. 1. Ed. Charles Plummer. Oxford: Oxford UP, 1896. 2 vols. 364-404. Eng. translation of abridged edition in Albertson 225-242.

_____. *Prose Life of St. Cuthbert.* In *Two Lives of Saint Cuthbert.* Ed. and trans. Bertram Colgrave. Cambridge: Cambridge UP, 1940. 142-307.

Cummian. *Epistola ad Segienum Huensem abbatem de Controversia Paschali.* PL 87.969-978.

Desiderius, Bishop of Cahors. *Epistolae.* PL 87.247-268.

Eadmer. *Vita Wilfridi.* In *Historians of the Church of York and its Archbishops.* Ed. James Raine. Vol. 1. Rolls Series 71. London, 1879. 3 vols. 161-226.

Earliest Life of Gregory the Great By an Anonymous Monk of Whitby. Ed. and trans. Bertram Colgrave. Lawrence, Kans.: U of Kansas P, 1968. Cambridge: Cambridge UP, 1985.

Eddius Stephanus. *The Life of Bishop Wilfrid.*
1)   In *Vita Wilfridi I. episcopi Eboracensis auctore Stephano.* Ed. Wilhelm Levison. MGH SRM 6. Hanover-Leipzig, 1913. 163-263.
2)   In *The Life of Bishop Wilfrid by Eddius Stephanus.* Ed. and trans. Bertram Colgrave. Cambridge: Cambridge UP, 1927.

Eusebius of Caesarea. *Ecclesiastical History.* Trans. Kirsopp Lake. 2 vols. Loeb Classical Library. Cambridge: Harvard UP, 1926.

Felix. *Life of St. Guthlac.* In *Felix's Life of St. Guthlac.* Ed. and trans. Bertram Colgrave. Cambridge: Cambridge UP, 1956.

Felix III, Pope. *Epistolae.* Ed. Andreas Thiel. *Epistolae Romanorum pontificum genuinae et quae ad eos scriptae sunt a S. Hilaro usque ad Pelagium II.* Braunsberg, E. Germany, 1867. Hildesheim, W. Germany: Georg Olms, 1974. 222-278.

Gregory the Great, Pope. *Dialogues.* Trans Odo John Zimmerman, O.S.B. Fathers of the Church 39. Washington, D.C.: Catholic UP, 1959.

Gregory of Tours, Bishop. *Liber vitae patrum.* Ed. Bruno Krusch. *Gregorii Turonensis Opera.* MGH SRM 1. Hanover: Hahn, 1885. 661-744.

_____. *Liber in gloria martyrum.* Ed. Bruno Krusch. *Gregorii Turonensis Opera.* MGH SRM 1. Hanover: Hahn, 1885. 484-561.

_____. *The History of the Franks.* Trans. Lewis Thorpe. Penguin Classics. Baltimore: Penguin Books, 1974.

Isidore of Seville. *De Ecclesiasticis Officiis.* PL 83.737-836.

Jerome. *Letter 1.* In *Select Letters of St. Jerome.* Ed. and trans. F. A. Wright. Loeb Classical Library 262. Cambridge, Mass.: Harvard UP, 1933. 2-19.

_____. *Liber Hebraicarum Quaestionum in Genesim.* PL 23.935-1010. Eng. trans. of Preface in *The Principal Works of St. Jerome.* Trans. W. H. Fremantle. A Select Library of the Nicene and Post-Nicene Fathers (Second Series) 6. Grand Rapids, Mich.: Wm. B. Eerdmans, 1954.

Justin Martyr. *Dialogue against Trypho.* In *The Apostolic Fathers: Justin Martyr - Irenaeus.* Ed. A. Cleveland Coxe. The Ante-Nicene Fathers 1. Grand Rapids, Michigan: Eerdmans, 1950. 194-272.

Lactantius. *The Deaths of the Persecutors.* In *Lactantius: The Minor Works.* Trans. Sister Mary Francis McDonald, O.P. Fathers of the Church 54. Washington, D.C.: The Catholic U of America P, 1965. 137-203.

Liber Pontificalis. In *Le Liber Pontificalis: texte, introduction et commentaire.* Ed. L. Duchesne. 2nd ed. Vol. 1. Paris: Boccard, 1955. 3 vols.

Mansi, Giovanni Domenico. *Sacrorum conciliorum nova et amplissima collectio.* 53 vols. Florence and Venice, 1759-98.

Martin I, Pope. *Epistolae.* PL 87.103-204.

Martyrdom of Polycarp. In *The Apostolic Fathers.* Ed. and trans. Kirsopp Lake. Vol. 2. Loeb Classical Library. London: William Heinemann, 1924. 2 vols. 307-345.

Maximus the Confessor. *Diffloratio ex epistola ejusdem s. Maximi ad Petrum illustrem.* In Anastasius *Collectanea.* PL 129.573-576.

Origen. *Homilies on Exodus.* In *Homilies on Genesis and Exodus.* Trans. Ronald E. Heine. Fathers of the Church 71. Washington, D.C.: Catholic U of America P, 1982.

Pseudo-Abdias [= *Acta Apostolorum Apocrypha . . . adscripta Abdiae*]. Ed. Johann Albert Fabricius. *Codex apocryphus Novi Testamenti.* Vol. 2. Hamburg, 1719. 3 vols. 388-742.

The Rule of St. Benedict. In *RB 1980: The Rule of St. Benedict in Latin and English with Notes.* Ed. Timothy Fry, O.S.B. Collegeville, Minnesota: Liturgical P, 1981.

The Rule of the Master. Trans. Luke Eberle. Intro. Adalbert de Vogüé. Cistercian Studies 6. Kalamazoo, Michigan: Cistercian Publications, 1977.

Sidonius Apollinaris. *Opera Omnia.* Ed. F. Leo and T. Mommsen. MGH AA 8. Berlin: Weidmann, 1887.

Stephen the Priest, s.v. "Eddius Stephanus."

Sulpicius Severus. *Dialogues.* In *The Western Fathers.* Trans. F. H. Hoare. London: Sheed and Ward, 1954. 68-144.

_____. *The Life of St. Martin.* In *The Western Fathers.* Trans. F. H. Hoare. London: Sheed and Ward, 1954. 10-44.

Tertullian. *Scorpiace.* In *Latin Christianity: Its Founder, Tertullian.* Ed. Alexander Roberts et al. Trans. S. Thelwall. American Edition. The Ante-Nicene Fathers 3. Grand Rapids, MI: Eerdmans, 1986. 633-648.

_____. *On Prescription Against Heretics.* In *Latin Christianity: Its Founder, Tertullian.* Ed. Alexander Roberts et al. Trans. Peter Holmes. American Edition. The Ante-Nicene Fathers 3. Grand Rapids, MI: Eerdmans, 1986. 243-265.

Theodore I, Pope. "Epistola Prima Synodica ad Paulum Patriarcham Constantinopolitanum." PL 87.75-80.

Thiel, Andreas, ed. *Epistolae Romanorum pontificum genuinae et quae ad eos scriptae sunt a S. Hilaro usque ad Pelagium II.* Braunsberg, Germany, 1867. Hildesheim, W. Germany: Georg Olms, 1974.

Victorius of Aquitaine. *Cursus Paschalis Annorum DXXXII.* Ed. Theodor Mommsen. MGH AA 9. Berlin: Weidmann, 1892. 677-684.

Modern Sources

"Abdias." *Dictionnaire des Apocryphes*. Ed. J. P. Migne. Paris, 1858. Vol. 24 of *Troisième et Dernière Encyclopédie Théologique*. 60 vols. 1858. 13-20.

Albertson, Clinton, ed. and trans. *Anglo-Saxon Saints and Heroes*. New York: Fordham UP, 1967.

Bréhier, Louis. "Les Colonies d'orientaux en occident au commencement du moyen-âge." *Byzantinische Zeitschrift* 12 (1903): 1-39.

Brown, Peter. *Augustine of Hippo*. Berkeley: U of California P, 1969.

_____. *The Cult of the Saints*. London: SCM, 1981.

Bury, J. B., H. M. Gwatkin, and J. P. Whitney, gen. eds. *The Rise of the Saracens and the Foundation of the Western Empire*. Cambridge: Cambridge UP, 1926. Vol. 2 of *Cambridge Medieval History*. 8 vols.

Campbell, James. "Bede." *Latin Historians*. Ed. T. A. Dorey. Studies in Latin and Its Influence. New York: Basic Books, 1966. 159-190.

_____, Eric John, and Patrick Wormald. *The Anglo-Saxons*. Ed. James Campbell. Ithaca, New York: Cornell UP, 1982.

Carte, Thomas. *A General History of England*. Vol. 1. London, 1747. 4 vols.

Clarke, H. B., and Mary Brennan, eds. *Columbanus and Merovingian Monasticism*. British Archaeological Reports, International Series 113. Oxford: British Archaeological Reports, 1981.

Colgrave, Bertram, ed. and trans. *Felix's Life of St. Guthlac*. Cambridge: Cambridge UP, 1956.

_____, ed. and trans. *Two Lives of Saint Cuthbert*. Cambridge: Cambridge UP, 1940.

_____, ed. and trans. *The Life of Bishop Wilfrid by Eddius Stephanus*. Cambridge: Cambridge UP, 1927.

_____. "Pilgrimages to Rome in the Seventh and Eighth Centuries." *Studies in Language, Literature, and Culture of the Middle Ages and Later*. Ed. E. Bagby Atwood and Archibald A. Hill. Austin, Texas: U of Texas, 1969.

_____, ed. and trans. *The Earliest Life of Gregory the Great By an Anonymous Monk of Whitby*. Lawrence, Kans.: U of Kansas P, 1968. Cambridge: Cambridge UP, 1985.

158

_____. "The Earliest Saints' Lives Written in England." *Proceedings of the British Academy* 44 (1958): 35-60.

Coville, Alfred. *Recherches sur l'histoire de Lyon du Vme au IXme siècle (450-800)*. Paris: Éditions Auguste Picard, 1928.

Dahl, Nils. "Amnesis: Memory and Commemoration in Early Christianity." *Studia Theologica* 1 (1948). Rpt. in *Jesus in the Memory of the Early Church*. Minneapolis: Augsburg Publishing House, 1976. 11-29.

Delehaye, Hippolyte. "L'Amphitheatre Flavien et ses environs dan les textes hagiographiques." *Analecta Bollandiana* 16 (1897): 236-248.

Diehl, Ernest, ed. *Inscriptiones Latinae Christianae Veteres*. Vol. 1. Berlin: Weidmann, 1925. 3 vols. Zurich: Weidmann, 1970.

Durliat, Jean. "Les Attributions civiles des évêques merovingiens: l'example de Didier, évêque de Cahors (630-655)." *Annales du Midi* 91 (1979): 237-254.

Eliade, Mircea. *The Myth of the Eternal Return*. Trans. Willard R. Trask. Bollingen Series 46. New York: Bollingen Foundation, 1965.

Ewig, Eugen. "Milo et Eiusmodi Similes." *Spätantikes und Fränkisches Gallien: Gesammelte Schriften (1952-1973)*. Ed. Hartmut Atsma. Vol. 2. Beihefte der Francia 3. Munich: Artemis, 1976. 2 vols. 189-219.

_____. "Kirche und Civitas in der Merowingerzeit." *Spätantikes und Fränkisches Gallien: Gesammelte Schriften (1952-1973)*. Ed. Hartmut Atsma. Vol. 2. Beihefte der Francia 3. Munich: Artemis, 1976. 2 vols. 1-20.

Fabricius, Johann Albert. *Codex Apocryphus Novi Testamenti*. Vol. 2. Hamburg, 1719. 3 vols.

Farmer, D. H. "Saint Wilfrid." *Saint Wilfrid at Hexham*. Ed. D. P. Kirby. Newcastle upon Tyne: Oriel P, 1974. 35-59.

Foley, William Trent. "*Imitatio Apostoli*: St. Wilfrid of York and the Andrew Script." *American Benedictine Review* 40 (1989): 13-31.

_____. "St. Wilfrid of York as *Pius Pater*: A Study of Late Roman Piety in Anglo-Saxon England." Diss. U of Chicago, 1984.

Fowler, Joseph T. *Memorials of the Church of SS. Peter and St. Wilfrid, Ripon*. Vol. 1. Surtees Society 74. Durham, 1882. 2 vols.

Frank, Karl S. "*Vita Apostolica*: Ansätze zur apostlischen Lebensform in der alten Kirche." *Zeitschrift für Kirchengeschichte* 82 (1981): 145-166.

Frend, W. H. C. *Martyrdom and Persecution in the Early Church.* New York: New York UP, 1967.

Gennep, Arnold van. *The Rites of Passage.* Trans. Monika B. Vizedom and Gabrielle Caffee. Chicago: U of Chicago P, 1960.

Godman, Peter, trans. and ed. *Alcuin: The Bishops, Kings, and Saints of York.* Oxford Medieval Texts. Oxford: Clarendon P, 1982.

Goffart, Walter. *The Narrators of Barbarian History (A.D. 550-800): Jordanes, Gregory of Tours, Bede and Paul the Deacon.* Princeton, N.J.: Princeton UP, 1988.

Gregg, Robert and Dennis Groh. *Early Arianism--A View of Salvation.* Philadelphia: Fortress P, 1980.

Hefele, Charles Joseph. *A History of the Councils of the Church.* Trans. William R. Clark. 5 vols. Edinburgh: T. & T. Clark, 1896. New York: AMS, 1972.

Heffernan, Thomas J. *Sacred Biography: Saints and Their Biographers in the Middle Ages.* New York: Oxford UP, 1988.

Heinzelmann, Martin. *Bischofsherrschaft in Gallien: zur Kontinuität römischer Fuhrungsschichten vom 4. bis 7. Jahrhunderts. Sociale, prosopographische und bildungsgeschichte Aspekte.* Beihefte der Francia 5. Munich: Artemis, 1976.

Hodgkin, R. H. *A History of the Anglo-Saxons.* 3rd ed. Vol. 1. London: Oxford UP, 1952. 2 vols.

Hodgkin, Thomas. *History of England from the Earliest Times to the Norman Conquest.* The Political History of England Ser. 1. London: Longmans, 1914.

Howe, Nicholas. *Migration and Mythmaking in Anglo-Saxon England.* New Haven: Yale UP, 1989.

Inett, John. *Origines Anglicanae; or a History of the English Church. Beginning where Bishop Stillingfleet has ended his 'History of the British Church.' And Containing An Account of the Affairs thereof, from the first planting of the Christian Religion amongst the English Saxons, till the Norman Conquest.* London, 1704. 2 vols.

Isenberg, Gabriele. *Die Würdigung Wilfrieds von York in der Historia Ecclesiastica gentis Anglorum Bedas und der Vita Wilfridi des Eddius.* Diss. Westfälischen Wilhelms-U. Münster: Weidenau/Sieg, 1978.

Jaffé, Philip, ed. *Regesta Pontificum Romanorum ab Condita Ecclesia ad Annum post Christum Natum MCXCVIII.* 2nd ed. 2 vols. Leipzig, 1885.

Jalland, Trevor Gervase. *The Church and Papacy: A Historical Study.* London: SPCK, 1944.

James, Montague Rhodes. *The Apocryphal New Testament.* Oxford: Clarendon Press, 1924.

James, Edward. "Bede and the Tonsure Question." *Peritia* 3 (1984): 85-98.

Johnson, Luke T. *The Writings of the New Testament: An Interpretation.* Philadelphia: Fortress Press, 1986.

Jones, A. H. M. *The Later Roman Empire, 284-602: A Social, Economic, and Administrative Survey.* Vol. 1. Oxford: Blackwell and Mott, 1964. 2 vols.

Käsemann, Ernst. "Is the Gospel Objective?" *Essays on New Testament Themes.* Trans. W. J. Montague. Studies in Biblical Theology 41, first ser. London: SCM, 1964. 48-62.

_____. "Paul and Early Catholicism." *New Testament Questions of Today.* Trans. W. J. Montague and Wilfred F. Bunge. Philadelphia: Fortress P, 1969. 236-251.

Keck, Leander E. *A Future for the Historical Jesus.* Nashville: Abingdon P, 1971.

Kelber, Werner H. *Mark's Story of Jesus.* Philadelphia: Fortress P, 1979.

Kelly, J. N. D. *The Oxford Dictionary of Popes.* Oxford: Oxford UP, 1986.

Kendrick T. D. et al. *Evangeliorum Quattuor Codex Lindisfarnensis, Musei Britannici Codex Cottonianus Nero....*2 vols. Lausanne, Switzerland: n. p., 1960.

Kierkegaard, Søren. *The Last Years: Journals, 1853-1855.* Ed. and trans. Ronald Gregor Smith. New York: Harper and Row, 1965.

Kirby, D. P. "Bede, Eddius Stephanus and the *Life of Wilfrid*." *English Historical Review* 98 (1983): 101-114.

_____. "Northumbria in the Time of Wilfrid." *Saint Wilfrid at Hexham.* Ed. D. P. Kirby. Newcastle-upon-Tyne: Oriel P, 1974. 1-34.

_____, ed. *Saint Wilfrid at Hexham.* Newcastle-upon-Tyne: Oriel P, 1974.

Krautheimer, Richard. *Rome: Profile of a City, 312-1308.* Princeton: Princeton UP, 1980.

Labriolle, Pierre de. "Papa." *Bulletin du Cange: Archivum Latinitatis Medii Aevi* 4 (1928): 65-75.

Levison, Wilhelm. *England and the Continent in the Eighth Century*. Oxford: Clarendon P, 1946.

_____, ed. *Vita Wilfridi I. episcopi Eboracensis auctore Stephano*. MGH SRM 6. Hanover-Leipzig, 1913. 163-263.

Llewellyn, P. A. B. "The Roman Church in the Seventh Century: The Legacy of Gregory I." *The Journal of Ecclesiastical History* 25 (1974): 363-380.

Lowe, E. A. *Codices Lugdunenses Antiquissimi: le scriptorium de Lyon, la plus ancienne école calligraphique de France*. Lyon: Bibliothèque de la ville de Lyon, 1924.

Malone, Edward E. *The Monk and the Martyr: The Monk as Successor of the Martyr*. The Catholic University of America Studies in Christian Antiquity 12. Washington, D.C.: Catholic U of America P, 1950.

_____. "The Monk and the Martyr." *Studia Anselmiana* 38 (1956): 201-228.

Mann, Horace K. *The Lives of the Popes in the Early Middle Ages*. Vol. 1. Part 1. London: Kegan Paul, 1902.

Mayr-Harting, Henry. *The Coming of Christianity to England*. New York: Schocken, 1972.

Moore, Stephen D. *Literary Criticism and the Gospels: The Theoretical Challenge*. New Haven: Yale UP, 1989.

Mordek, Hubert. *Kirchenrecht und Reform im Frankenreich: die "Collectio Vetus Gallica," die älteste systematische Kanonessammlung des Frankischen Gallien--Studien und Edition*. Beiträge zur Geschichte und Quellenkunde des Mittelalters 1. Berlin: Walter de Gruyter, 1975.

Nelson, Janet. "Queens as Jezebels: the Careers of Brunhild and Balthild in Merovingian History." *Medieval Women*. Ed. Derek Baker. Studies in Church History, Subsidia 1. Oxford: Blackwell, 1978. 31-77.

Neuhäuser, Engelbert. *Der Bischof als geistlicher Vater nach den frühchristlichen Schriften*. Munich: Kösel Verlag, 1964.

Niebuhr, H. Richard. *The Meaning of Revelation*. New York: Macmillan, 1967.

Patte, Daniel, and Aline Patte. *Structural Exegesis: From Theory to Practice*. Philadelphia: Fortress Press, 1978.

Patte, Daniel. *Paul's Faith and the Power of the Gospel: A Structural Introduction to the Pauline Letters*. Philadelphia: Fortress, 1983.

Perrin, Norman. *The New Testament: An Introduction.* New York: Harcourt, 1974.

Plummer, Charles. *Venerabilis Baedae Opera Historica.* Vol. 2: Commentary and indices. Oxford: Oxford UP, 1896. 2 vols.

Poole, Reginald Lane. "St Wilfrid and the See of Ripon." *Studies in Chronology and History.* Oxford: Clarendon P, 1934. 56-81.

Prinz, Friedrich. *Frühes Mönchtum im Frankenreich: Kultur under Gesellschaft in Gallien, den Rheinlanden und Bayern am Beispiel der monastischen Entwicklung (4. bis 8. Jahrhundert).* Munich: R. Oldenbourg, 1965.

_____. "Die bischöfliche Stadtherrschaft im Frankenreich vom 5. bis 7. Jahrhundert." *Historische Zeitschrift* 217.1 (1973): 1-35.

Richards, Jeffrey. *The Popes and Papacy in the Early Middle Ages.* London: Routledge and Kegan Paul, 1979.

Riedinger, Rudolf. "Zwei Briefe aus den Akten der Lateransynode von 649." *Jahrbuch der Osterreichischen Byzantinistik* 29 (1980): 37-59.

Roper, Michael. "The Territorial Possessions of St. Wilfrid and Their Influence upon His Career." M.A. Thesis. U of Manchester, England, 1958.

_____. "Wilfrid's Landholdings in Northumbria." *Saint Wilfrid at Hexham.* Ed. D. P. Kirby. Newcastle-upon-Tyne: Oriel P, 1974. 61-79.

Rossi, Giovanni Battista de. *La Roma sotterranea cristiana descritta ed illustrata.* Vol. 1. Rome, 1864-1897. 4 vols.

_____. *Inscriptiones Christianae urbis Romae septimo saeculo antiqiores.* Vol. 2. Rome: Officina Libraria Pontifica, 1857-1861. 2 vols.

Rush, Alfred C. "Spiritual Martyrdom in St. Gregory the Great." *Theological Studies* 23 (1962): 569-589.

Ryan, John. *Irish Monasticism: Origins and Early Development.* London: Longmans, Green, 1931.

Shils, Edward. "Charisma, Order, and Status." *American Sociological Review* 30 (1965): 199f. Rpt. in *The Constitution of Society.* The Heritage of Sociology. Chicago: U of Chicago P, 1972. 119-142.

Stancliffe, Clare. *St. Martin and His Hagiographer: History and Miracle in Sulpicius Servus.* Oxford: Clarendon P, 1983.

Stenton, Frank M. *Anglo-Saxon England.* 3rd ed. Oxford History of England. Oxford: Oxford UP, 1971.

Stokes, Whitney, and Strachan, John, eds. *Thesaurus Palaeohibernicus: A Collection of Old Irish Glosses, Scholia, Prose and Verse.* 2 vols. Cambridge: Cambridge UP, 1901-03.

Stubbs, William. *The Constitutional History of England in Its Origins and Development.* 6th ed. Vol. 1. Oxford: Clarendon, 1897. New York: Barnes, 1967. 3 vols.

Tillich, Paul. *Theology of Culture.* Ed. Robert C. Kimball. 1959. London: Oxford UP, 1975.

———. *The Dynamics of Faith.* World Perspectives 10. New York: Harper, 1957.

Turner, Victor. *Dramas, Fields and Metaphors: Symbolic Action in Human Society.* Ithaca, New York: Cornell UP, 1974.

———. *Process, Performance and Pilgrimage.* Ranchi Anthropological Ser. 1. New Delhi: Concept Publishing Co., 1979.

———., and Edith Turner. *Image and Pilgrimage in Christian Culture: Anthropological Perspectives.* Oxford: Blackwell, 1978.

Ullmann, Walter. *The Growth of Papal Government in the Middle Ages: A Study in the Ideological Relation of Clerical to Lay Power.* London: Methuen, 1955.

Ward, Benedicta, S.L.G. "The Spirituality of St Cuthbert." *St. Cuthbert and His Cult and His Community to A.D. 1200.* Ed. Gerald Bonner, David Rollason, and Clare Stancliffe. Woodbridge, Suffolk: Boydell and Brewer, 1989. 65-76.

Whitelock, Dorothy. "Bede and His Teachers and Friends." *Famulus Christi: Essays in Commemoration of the Thirteenth Centenary of the Birth of the Venerable Bede.* Ed. Gerald Bonner. London: SPCK, 1976. 19-39.

———, ed. *C. 597-1042.* Vol. 1 of *English Historical Documents.* Gen. ed. David C. Douglas. 2nd ed. 12 vols. London: Eyre, 1979.

Wormald, Patrick. "Bede, *Beowulf,* and the Conversion of Anglo-Saxon England." *Bede and Anglo-Saxon England.* Ed. Robert Thomas Farrell. British Archaeological Reports 46. Oxford: British Archaeological Reports, 1978. 32-95.

Zwölfer, Theodor. *Sankt Peter, Apostelfürst und Himmelspförtner: seine Verehrung bei den Angelsachsen und Franken.* Stuttgart: W. Kohlhammer, 1929.

INDEX

Carte, Thomas: 3 n. 3, 37 n. 19, 130

Centwini, king of Wessex: 43

Chad, bishop of Northumbria and Mercia: 73, 76-77, 86, 88, 105

Clotar III, king of Burgundy: 84, 101

Ceolred, king of Mercia: 56 n. 3, 62

Colgrave, Bertram: 34 n. 16

Collectio Vetus Gallica: 122

Columba, St., of Iona: 103

confessor (see types): apostle as, 42; monk as, 42; Stephen's Wilfrid as, 17, 33, 43-44, 47, 110-111; Cuthbert as, 42-43, 110

Constantine I, Emperor: 79, 89; convictions, religious: nature of, 3-5, 10; in *Life of Wilfrid*, 6, 8

Constans II, Emperor: 87

Cudda: 55, 58

Cummian: 116

Cuthbert, St., bishop of Lindisfarne: 16, 76-77, 103, 105, 118; as "secret martyr", 77; compared with Wilfrid, 74, 88, 107-109, 123, 125-126; cult of, 15-16, 125; death of, 109-110; earliest Lives of, 16, 27-28, 42-43, 73; *Anonymous Life*'s portrayal of, 1-2, 41-42, 73, 110-114, 119-121, 128; Bede's portrayal of, 88 n. 26, 128

Dagobert I, king of the Franks: 56 n. 3, 66 n

Dalfinus (see also Annemundus, archbishop of Lyon): 30-32, 33, 34 n. 16, 44, 56, 58, 60, 61, 65, 65 n. 12, 111; relations with Wilfrid, 55, 65; his identification with Annemundus, 30 n. 11; martyrdom of, 32

Desiderius, archbishop of Cahors: 17, 90

Deusdedit, Pope: 100

Eadwulf, king of Northumbria: 38